» Living Stories of the Cherokee

›› Líving Storíes

Foreword by
Joyce Conseen Dugan,
Principal Chief,
Eastern Band of
Cherokee Indians

f the Cherokee

With stories told by
Davey Arch,
Robert Bushyhead,
Edna Chekelelee,
Marie Junaluska,
Kathi Smith Littlejohn,
and Freeman Owle

Collected and edited by

Barbara R. Duncan

The University of
North Carolina Press

Chapel Hill & London

© 1998 The University of North Carolina Press

All rights reserved

Designed by April Leidig-Higgins

Set in Joanna by Keystone Typesetting, Inc.

Manufactured in the United States of America

Library of Congress Cataloging-in-Publication Data

Living stories of the Cherokee / collected and edited
by Barbara R. Duncan with stories told by Davey
Arch . . . [et al.].

p.   cm.

Includes biblographical references and index.

ISBN 0-8078-2411-9 (cloth: alk. paper).

ISBN 0-8078-4719-4 (pbk.: alk. paper)

1. Cherokee Indians—Folklore. 2. Tales—North
Carolina. 3. Storytellers—North Carolina.
I. Duncan, Barbara R. II. Arch, Davey.

E99.C5L55   1998   97-35037

398.2'089'9755—dc21   CIP

Pages 10, 11, 29, 143, 189: Photographs by
Barbara Duncan. Pages 12, 75, 193:
Photographs by Ron Ruehl. Page 125:
Photograph by Barbara Lau.

02 01 00 99 98   5 4 3 2 1

GWY DƟYD

(Literally, "Cherokee, they are saying")

>> Contents

➤➤ **Robert Bushyhead** 143

➤➤ **Marie Junaluska** 189

➤➤ **Freeman Owle** 193

>> Foreword

Many have written about our history and culture. Few of these people have come from our community, with the traditional knowledge and understanding of what it means to be a Cherokee. Our storytellers have grown to appreciate the knowledge and understanding vital to our continuation as a People. This work is important for that reason. Barbara Duncan has been a part of our community long enough to understand what it means for us to have an opportunity to tell our own stories—not recited from a history text but told through the voices of our members.

In the work you are about to read, you will see how Barbara has come into our community and grown to become a scholar committed to providing the Cherokee storytellers with a voice. This voice could have been provided by others, but probably none who walk among us as our friend; often it is provided by those who feel the right to tell these legends as their own. Barbara has worked toward helping the outside world understand that these legends are important because they belong to Cherokees, not because someone outside our community can recite them.

Through the years, these legends have grown and changed and become contemporary along with Cherokee people. You may have heard these legends on cassette tape. Soon you may hear them via computer, and in the next millennium we can only guess the media through which you will experience these stories. The critical message is that the stories continue. We have often looked toward our neighbors to help us with problems, and it is indeed a pleasure to find help in preserving our traditions as well.

I hope you will enjoy this work as much as I have, and that you will continue our tradition of sharing these legends with your family and friends. The voices you hear are those of my friends and neighbors, and now they become yours.

Joyce Conseen Dugan
Principal Chief
Eastern Band of Cherokee Indians
September 1997

>> Acknowledgments

Thanks to the Tribal Council of the Eastern Band of the Cherokee for giving their approval to this project. Thanks also to Lynn Harlan, Cultural Officer for the Eastern Band, for helpful conversations.

During the process of writing this book I was working on two other Cherokee projects for the Museum of the Cherokee Indian: a documentary video on the history of the Eastern Band and a new permanent exhibit for the museum. Both of these projects were collaborations between the Cherokee people and scholars of the Cherokee. In the process, much information was shared, and this book has benefited from all of our conversations and work together.

Thanks to Ken Blankenship, director of the museum, for involving me in the process of the new permanent exhibit, and thanks to Ron Ruehl for involving me in the production of The Principal People, a documentary video, and for allowing me to combine research for the video and the storytelling book. I hope that the reader who enjoys this book and wants to know more about the Cherokee will seek out both the video and the new museum exhibit. The video, the exhibit, and, I hope, this book will help to acquaint the public with the history, the culture, and the worldview of the Cherokee.

Thanks to the storytellers: Davey Arch, Robert Bushyhead, Edna Chekelelee, Kathi Smith Littlejohn, and Freeman Owle. Thanks to Marie Junaluska, translator, and to Jean Blanton, daughter of Robert

Bushyhead. The storytellers have been paid for their contributions to the book, and a portion of the royalties will be donated to nonprofit organizations on the Qualla Boundary.

In addition to the storytellers featured in this book, an equal number of Eastern Cherokee people are recognized by the Cherokee community as important public storytellers including: Lloyd Arneach, whose commitments did not allow him to be included in this collection; Freddie Bradley, who tells stories as part of his job with the National Park Service in Gatlinburg, Tennessee; Driver Pheasant, who works for the Museum of the Cherokee Indian in educational outreach; Tom Hill, a new storyteller; and others who are just beginning to be known as storytellers.

Thanks to my friends and colleagues for essential and helpful conversations: Henry Glassie at Indiana University, Tom McGowan at Appalachian State University, Margaret Mills at the University of Pennsylvania, Glenn Hinson at the University of North Carolina at Chapel Hill, Sally Peterson at the North Carolina Museum of History, Duane King at the Southwestern Museum (who also told a version of "The Belt That Would Not Burn"), Joan Greene at the Museum of the Cherokee Indian, John Finger at the University of Tennessee, Anne Rogers and William Anderson at Western Carolina University, attorney Ben Bridgers in Sylva, North Carolina, and Mary Chiltoskey and Jean Jackson from Cherokee.

Thanks to the North Carolina Arts Council for permission to quote from interviews with Rev. Robert Bushyhead and his daughter Jean Bushyhead Blanton. Thanks to Peggy Bulger and the Southern Arts Federation for sharing videotape of Edna Chekelelee's performance in the Sisters of the South tour. Thanks to the Qualla Arts and Crafts Co-op for sharing videotape of the speakers' bureau workshop with storytelling. Thanks to the Museum of the Cherokee Indian and Ron Ruehl for permission to use videotaped material for some versions of stories.

Thanks to David Perry, Elaine Maisner, and Pam Upton at the University of North Carolina Press for their support and understanding through this process. Thanks to my sister, Susan Reimensnyder, for help with Internet research and transcription.

Thanks to my friend Hawk Littlejohn, for sharing his knowledge of Cherokee culture with me over the years and for being my friend. Thanks to my husband, John Duncan, for his support and to my two children, John Harper and Pearl, for sharing their mama with this book—your love makes everything possible. Thanks to the Creator.

>> Living Stories of the Cherokee

>> Introduction

Cherokee culture is alive in the hearts of the Cherokee people. It is stronger, richer, bigger, and more enduring than any book that can be written about it. Storytelling is part of Cherokee culture, and it, too, is alive and strong. Cherokee people have always told stories to their children, among their families, and in their community, but in recent years, Cherokee storytellers have begun to share stories with the general public at events outside the Cherokee community. This book presents several contemporary storytellers who are members of the Eastern Band of Cherokee Indians, located in western North Carolina. Kathi Littlejohn, Davey Arch, Edna Chekelelee, Robert Bushyhead, and Freeman Owle all grew up hearing stories from their families and from the community, and they learned to tell stories in that traditional setting. All of them, however, have also become skilled at telling stories in schools, in seminars, in workshops, and at festivals; it is their willingness to share Cherokee tales with the larger world that has made this book possible. Marie Junaluska has contributed a translation into Cherokee of one tale, with phonetic transcription and syllabary.

What makes this book unique is its focus on collecting stories that are being told today by living storytellers. It is the first major collection of Eastern Band stories to be widely published in almost a hundred years, since James Mooney's *Myths of the Cherokee* first appeared in 1900.

The Cherokee have lived in western North Carolina for thousands of years. Archaeologists have found artifacts near the spring on Wayah Bald and in other places dating back to 9000 B.C. The Cherokee have most likely told stories for the many years that they have lived in these mountains. The 11,000-year-old artifacts on the mountain could have been left by the ancestors of the Cherokee, and their stories could have been the ancestors of these stories.

Every culture in the world, from the Stone Age to the Space Age, has stories, music, humor, and spiritual ceremonies. Stories like the Gilgamesh epic from ancient Persia have existed in written and oral tradition, we know, for about five thousand years. The Bible has long been part of written and oral Judeo-Christian tradition—six thousand years for parts of the Old Testament and two thousand years for the New Testament. Cherokee stories could be this old. Stories endure.

But every culture, every story, is only one generation away from extinction. Stories die, simply and quietly, when no one thinks they're important enough to take the time to tell. Stories can be preserved only by being included in living tradition.

My hope is not to "save" stories from extinction, but to let people know that these stories are wonderful and important. I hope that future generations of Cherokee storytellers continue to find them so. This work celebrates the fact that the stories it presents—and many others—continue to exist in oral tradition a hundred years after James Mooney listened to them. In its pages the world at large can discover these wonderful, wise, funny stories still told by members of the Eastern Band, still living on their ancestral homeland. In their small community, both the stories and the storytellers are alive and abundant.

In order to convey to the reader the fundamental oral nature of these tales and their beauty as they are told, they are presented on the page word for word exactly as they were spoken. Because the storytellers tell their tales in a rhythmic way, the stories are transcribed in lines of different lengths, like free verse, indicating pauses in the teller's speech. If you read them aloud, or listen to them in your mind, you will hear the stories as the storytellers speak them. Folklorists have been using this way of presenting stories, called oral poetics, since the 1970s to convey the voices of the people. When stories are rewritten to be more literary and "readable," they lose the beauty and style of the oral versions and their tellers, whose voices are drowned out by the conventions of standard English and the changes of the editor.

Each of the main sections of the book is devoted to one storyteller, introduced by a short headnote containing biographical information and interesting comments on specific stories provided by the tellers themselves. The storytellers include men and women of all ages. Their stories and styles are all different.

The book begins with Kathi Littlejohn, a young woman who tells tales in an entertaining and dramatic style. Employed by the tribe as Director of Health and Human Services, Kathi does most of her storytelling in schools. She has produced two cassette tapes and would like to teach more children to tell stories.

Davey Arch is also young, but his repertoire includes more personal-experience narratives, especially stories about his grandfather, who was born early in the twentieth century and followed a very traditional lifestyle, living in the old Cherokee way. Davey also tells some of the stories he learned from his grandfather. A talented carver of masks, Davey speaks to many groups, demonstrates carving, and tells stories. Some of his masks depict events from the stories.

Edna Chekelelee, who recently passed away at the age of sixty-five, came from an older generation of storytellers. Unlike Kathi and Davey, Edna grew up speaking the Cherokee language and was as fluent in Cherokee as she was in English. Although she knew many old folktales about animals and ghosts and many stories describing historical events, later in life, as she began performing more in public, her stories took on the form you see here—short, poetic, humorous, and to the point. Edna came from the isolated Snowbird community, part of the Cherokee lands located in Graham County near Robbinsville, North Carolina.

Reverend Robert Bushyhead also comes from an older generation of storytellers and grew up speaking the Cherokee language. He spent his adult life as a traveling missionary for the Baptist Church, and when he retired to Cherokee, North Carolina, he began performing in the outdoor drama Unto These Hills. He has dedicated the past several years to documenting, along with his daughter Jean B. Blanton, the Kituwah dialect of the Cherokee language and creating textbooks, videos, and other study materials to be used in the Cherokee schools. His lifelong interest in language and oratory are reflected in the style and content of his stories. He speaks in long lines with beautiful cadences, and his story about Mrs. Lee has the formal structure and development of a literary short story. His subjects are religion and Cherokee medicine, his experiences as a native speaker, and Sequoyah, who invented the written Cherokee syllabary in the early 1800s. In 1996 Bushyhead was awarded both the North Carolina Folk Heritage Award and the Mountain Heritage Award in recognition of his work with the Cherokee language. A group of elders meets monthly at his house to share stories and memories in the Cherokee language.

Marie Junaluska is one of the few members of the younger generation who grew up speaking Cherokee. Recognized as an outstanding translator, she was recently elected to the Tribal Council. She has translated original articles from the *Cherokee Phoenix* newspaper into English and has worked as a language and culture teacher in the Cherokee schools. Marie has translated into written Cherokee two well-known stories from James Mooney's collection. One of them, "The Origin of the Milky Way," appears in this volume. The reader can see here the Cherokee language as it appears on the page, each symbol representing a syllable. Sequoyah, who spent twelve years devising the syllabary, is the only individual in history known to have created a system of written language without first being literate himself. At a tribal council meeting in 1821, Sequoyah and his daughter Ayoka gave a dramatic demonstration of the syllabary. The council approved Sequoyah's system, and nearly all tribal members became literate within a year.

The stories of Freeman Owle end this collection. One of the younger generation whose first language is English, Freeman tells many of the classic myths of the Cherokee. A former schoolteacher, he now speaks to many groups about Cherokee culture and has continued his own historical and cultural researches. When performing in the southern Appalachians, he often weaves historical fact and stories about the particular location of the storytelling event into his evening's discourse, taking listeners to another world once located where they are now sitting.

Animal stories, creation myths, legends, ghost stories, stories about places, and stories about family members are included in the repertoires. Some will easily be recognized as myths ("How the World Was Made") and legends ("The Legend of the Pileated Woodpecker"). Others are specific to families and individuals; these are included because they are part of family folklore and because they have been told for a very long time, although they may vary from generation to generation. Stories about healing, about supernatural experiences, about grandfathers and grandmothers, about particular places in the mountains—these are all traditional stories just as much as is "How the Possum Lost His Tail."

Most books of Cherokee stories on the market today are literary retellings from Mooney's collection, which is still a classic, monumental work. A few scholars have collected stories and other cultural materials on the Qualla Boundary, the 57,000 acres owned by the Eastern Band and held in trust by the federal government, located sixty miles west of Asheville in the rugged Smoky Mountains of western North Carolina. Frans Olbrechts collected in Big Cove in 1926–27 and finished Mooney's *Swimmer Manuscript* for the Bureau of American Ethnology (1932). Jack and Anna Kilpatrick published some Cherokee stories from Olbrechts's notes in the Bureau of American Ethnology's annual reports in 1966. *Friends of Thunder*, their collection of stories from the Cherokee Nation in Oklahoma, has been published by the University of Oklahoma Press. And retired schoolteacher Mary Ulmer Chiltoskey, a white woman from Alabama who married Cherokee woodcarver Going Back Chiltoskey, has actively collected and retold many stories in western North Carolina, publishing a number of them in pamphlet form.

By focusing, as this book does, on storytellers and stories alive in oral tradition today, we learn that Cherokee storytelling is a living, vital tradition hundreds, perhaps thousands, of years old, valued both within the community and by outsiders. Tales collected by James Mooney more than a hundred years ago still exist in oral tradition, though at the time Mooney feared that the traditions were dying out. Many traditional stories circulate in addition to those that were documented by Mooney. Cherokee storytelling grows and changes as new tales are added and old ones are changed or forgotten. New stories about recent events and family histories form an important part of oral tradition along with the animal stories, creation myths, and legends. For example, Freeman Owle tells a story about his great-great-grandfather and the Trail of Tears, and many families on the Qualla Boundary still tell stories about what happened to their ancestors during the Removal.

Cherokee storytelling, at least in its public forms, has changed from being presented mainly in the Cherokee language to being mainly in English, but it is still distinctly Cherokee. Traditional stories and values have survived changes in language and in the outward form of the culture. Cherokee people drive cars and live in modern houses, but the use of modern technology doesn't necessarily mean the loss of traditional culture. Values, stories, and ideas have a reality of their own.

›› History of the Eastern Band of Cherokee Indians

The Eastern Band includes about ten thousand people, most of whom live on a small part of the ancestral Cherokee homelands in the mountains of western North Carolina. Their present home, the Qualla Boundary, includes 57,000 acres of mountains, streams, and coves owned by the Eastern Band and held in trust by the federal government. The Eastern Band legally has "deferred sovereignty status," meaning that the people live and govern themselves as a sovereign nation within the United States. They have the power to make and enforce their own laws, providing these do not conflict with certain federal laws, such as those concerning homicide.

The Eastern Band was once part of the much larger Cherokee nation, which in the early 1700s spread over 140,000 acres, with seventy-two major towns. The Cherokee sited their villages on bottomlands along the rivers and hunted through the heights, covering territory in Georgia, North Carolina, east Tennessee, upper South Carolina, and parts of Alabama, Virginia, Kentucky, and West Virginia—the area we know today as the southern Appalachians and foothills.

By the early nineteenth century, the federal government, seeking land in the Southeast for expansion, began planning to remove the Cherokee and the other four "civilized tribes"—the Creek, Choctaw, Chickasaw, and Seminole—from the Southeast. These plans were controversial and were hotly debated throughout the country. The Cherokee nation sent to Washington, D.C., a petition opposing Removal and signed by more than sixteen thousand tribal members; Ralph Waldo Emerson wrote a personal letter to President Martin Van Buren decrying the concept; Congressman and American legend David Crockett of Tennessee voted against Removal. However, the bill for Removal passed Congress by one vote in May 1836.

At the time of Removal, the Cherokee nation numbered more than twenty thousand men, women, and children. It had a constitutional government, its own language, and a bilingual newspaper (in Cherokee and English), the Cherokee Phoenix. The Cherokee were farmers and plantation owners whose children were educated in mission schools, who owned slaves on some plantations in north Georgia, and who were, in terms of using technology, as "civilized" as their white neighbors. Many were Christians. Although in 1830 the Supreme Court had upheld the status of the Cherokee as a nation within the state of Georgia, the decision was disregarded by then-President Andrew Jackson, and plans went forward for Removal, which was approved by Congress in 1836 and carried out in 1838.

The Cherokee were rounded up at gunpoint, held in stockades for several months, and then marched to Oklahoma on what became known as the Trail of Tears. Estimates of casualties for the whole process—removal, imprisonment, march, and the first year in Oklahoma—range as high as eight to ten thousand. Scholars agree that at least four thousand perished on the trail itself.

Some Cherokee were able to remain in North Carolina, however, and from that circumstance comes both a legend and some information of historical interest. The legend says that Tsali, a Cherokee man, was taken at gunpoint from his home along with his wife and older sons. On the way to the stockade, an incident involving Tsali's wife caused Tsali and his sons to react violently; they killed two soldiers and then fled into the woods. They eluded capture but were finally approached by William Holland Thomas, a white man raised by Yonaguska (Drowning Bear), with a bargain: If Tsali and his sons would turn themselves in for execution, the soldiers would allow the rest of the Cherokee people who were hiding the mountains to remain there. Tsali agreed, he and his sons came in and were shot (except for the youngest, who was spared because of his age), and the Cherokee hiding in the mountains were allowed to remain in western North Carolina, forming the nucleus of today's Eastern Band.

This story is known to many Cherokee people and has been performed for millions of visitors in the outdoor drama *Unto These Hills*. Along with family stories about Removal, this is an important tale for the Cherokee people, one that exemplifies the importance of putting the good of the whole ahead of personal good. It is a story of sacrifice and survival that sums up the heartbreak of the Removal. And, in historical fact, when Tsali and his sons were executed, the U.S. Army ceased to hunt any more Cherokee "fugitives."

For the sake of historical accuracy, it is important to note that in addition to the Cherokee people who hid in the mountains during Removal and those who went to Oklahoma and then simply turned around and came back, there were a number of Cherokees who neither hid nor were removed: the Oconaluftee Citizen Indians. About sixty Cherokee families had been granted 640 acres of land each under the provisions of the federal treaties of 1817 and 1819. North Carolina was the only state to honor these provisions, upholding them in court in 1827 in a case brought by Yonaguska's daughter. As a result, about 38,000 acres were held by this group, which lived in the present-day counties of Cherokee, Graham, Macon, and Swain.

One of the leaders of the Oconaluftee group was Yonaguska, who in 1830 had a vision telling him to teach the people to avoid alcohol and to remain in their homeland. The Oconaluftee Cherokee heeded this advice and by the time of the Removal had gained a reputation for being temperate and hardworking; several North Carolina legislators even testified to that effect in the state general assembly, in support of the Oconaluftees' request to remain in North Carolina at the time of Removal. Their request was approved by the state of North Carolina.

The Oconaluftee Citizen Indians, as they were known, along with those Cherokee who hid in the mountains and those who returned almost immediately from Oklahoma, became the grandfathers and grandmothers of today's Eastern Band. The land owned by the Oconaluftee Indians, augmented by purchases of land through Will Thomas, became part of today's 57,000-acre Qualla Boundary.

The presence of the Oconaluftee Citizen Indians helps to explain a number of other Cherokee family stories from the time of Removal. Such narratives describe ancestors who traveled on the Trail of Tears but escaped along the way to return to North Carolina, like Kathi Smith Littlejohn's mother-in-law's grandmother. One tells about Junaluska, Edna Chekelelee's great-grandfather's brother, who walked all the way to Oklahoma and then turned around and walked back to North Carolina. He is buried in Robbinsville, where his grave is marked off by an iron fence. Other stories refer to Cherokee people who hid in caves and were helped by white people "until it was safe to come out." Still others describe people like Freeman Owle's great-great-grandparents, who worked for white farmers until they raised enough money so that Will Thomas could buy land for them. While the kindness of white neighbors no doubt helped Cherokee people survive, these stories make more sense in the knowledge that there was a settled community of Cherokee people still in the mountains who would have been able to help returning relatives.

Ironically, although the members of this community were known as "citizen" Indians, they were citizens of neither the United States nor the state of North Carolina. The treaty provisions allowed them to "apply" for citizenship, a process that required, among other criteria, a petition with the signatures of fifty white men for each Cherokee. The Eastern Cherokee's citizenship remained in limbo until 1946, although they paid North Carolina state taxes and were drafted for military service under federal laws. Despite the efforts of veterans returning after World War I and of women following the adoption of suffrage in 1920, the Eastern Cherokee were not allowed to register to vote until 1946, when veterans of World War II finally prevailed on local registrars.

›› Stories and Cultural Identity

The Eastern Cherokee have survived physically, living on a portion of their ancient territory. They have survived culturally as well, speaking the Kituwah dialect of the Cherokee language, making traditional pots, baskets, and other crafts, and telling Cherokee stories. Every culture's stories and language make that culture unique. For Europeans, beginning in the nineteenth century, language and folklore became crucial elements in defining national identity. The Grimms' folktales and language studies gave the Germans something to point to while saying: "These stories make us German."

9

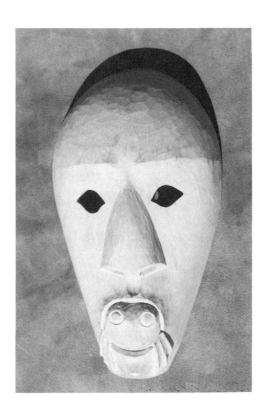

Davey Arch mask illustrating "The Strange Husband"

Likewise, the Cherokee can say, "This language, our syllabary, and these stories make us Cherokee." The Cherokee have had much in common with their southeastern neighbors the Creeks, the Catawbas, and others, but their language, their stories, their stamped pottery, their blowguns, and their winter houses all contributed to their uniqueness. The Cherokee always assumed that language was synonymous with tribal identity. This assumption ran so deep that, during the Revolutionary War, they were perplexed that people who all spoke English would make war against each other.

▸▸ Stories and the Arts

Cherokee stories are interwoven not only with Cherokee language but also with history, dances, songs, medicine, and arts and crafts. Freeman Owle tells of his great-great-grandfather's experience during the Removal as though it happened yesterday. Before she dances,

Davey Arch mask illustrating "The Old Man and the Blowgun"

Edna Chekelelee tells the story of how the Quail Dance came to be. When she tells stories from the Trail of Tears, holding a basket that was carried on the trail and brought back, she sings the song that the people sang when they first arrived in Oklahoma, "Oh How I Love Jesus." Davey Arch tells the story of his grandfather's treatment by Mink, a famous medicine man at the turn of the century. Animals interact with conjure men and women in Kathi Smith Littlejohn's tales about why the mole lives underground and how the pileated woodpecker came to be. Davey Arch carves masks that illustrate his stories, like the mask with a frog coming out of a man's mouth, illustrating "The Strange Husband." Another of his masks shows a bird flying out of a man's mouth, something that happens in "The Old Man and the Blowgun." Freeman Owle carves stone into animal figures or collections of images that represent his stories. Conversely, stories may also explain the origins of arts and crafts such as pottery, as in "Me-Li and the Mud Dauber."

Freeman Owle stone carving

For the Cherokee, culture and traditions create a holistic experience, as they do for all peoples. As another example, in popular American culture a European folktale may be transformed into a Walt Disney film, which in turn generates mass-produced clothing, books, songs, and toys.

›› Stories and Education

Cherokee stories were and continue to be used consciously to educate children in cultural values and to reaffirm those values for adults. As Freeman Owle has said, "Each and every story had a real reason for it. The Cherokees did not have schools, so they had to tell stories to teach their children." This teaching included moral values as well as the history of the people. One of the most often-told animal stories, "How the Possum Lost His Tail," has this moral: Do not brag about your abilities or you will get in trouble. This is how the possum lost his tail; it is also how the brave and mighty warrior ended up being killed with his own weapons.

We also learn that it is bad to be greedy; greed allows the Rabbit to trick the Fox out of his string of fish. We learn that the evil you do will come back against you, as happened in "The Old Man and the Birds" when the thief who stole the old man's food starved to death himself. We learn that those who are different have something important to contribute, like the bat who wins "The Birds and Animals Stickball Game." We learn that we are related to all the plants, animals, and spirits, like "Forever Boy" in Kathi Littlejohn's story "The Cherokee Little People." We learn that the Creator, the Little People, and the Nunnehi (the spirit people) can help us if we ask them properly. In learning all these lessons, we also learn the place of a Cherokee person in relationship to the rest of the world. If you are a Cherokee child hearing these stories, you learn all these things, and above all you learn what it means to be Cherokee.

›› Stories and History

Some stories tell the history of the people, like those about the Trail of Tears or about events in the "old days." Some are family stories, like Freeman Owle's narrative about what happened to his great-great-grandfather during Removal and how his family was able to continue to live in North Carolina.

Many families tell stories about how they came to be part of the Eastern Band instead of being taken to Oklahoma in the Removal. Although these events happened in 1838, they are told as though they happened yesterday. Solomon Bird, who lives in Robbinsville, can point to the place in the road in front of his house where soldiers rounded up his grandmother, with her grandparents, when she was a little girl in 1838. The events of more than 150 years ago can pass from a grandmother to her grandson, and from the grandson to his own grandchild, in only two tellings. These two tellings can precisely convey the facts and emotions of events. Stories, the seeds of history and culture and identity, can pass through two tellers over a century and a half and still bear fruit that will grow true to seed, like Cherokee corn.

›› Stories and Origins

No one knows how old these stories are. Some tell about the origin of corn and beans, and archaeologists say that the Cherokee began growing corn sometime before 500 A.D. and beans sometime before 1200 A.D. Perhaps the origin stories could be placed within that timeframe. Walker Calhoun has said his grandmother told a tale about a "giant lizard" that could have referred to the dinosaurs or other ancient creatures. Other stories, collected by James Mooney, refer to unknown beasts such as the giant yellow jacket that nested at Standing Indian in Macon County or the giant leech that lived near the conjunction of the Hiawassee and Valley Rivers near present-day Murphy, North Carolina. Although references to unknown animals do not tell us the age of the story, they may suggest a much earlier time when these animals might have roamed the mountains, with stories of them living well beyond their extinction.

Archaeologists agree that the ancestors of the Cherokee exhibited unique, identifiable cultural characteristics as early as 250 A.D., including the production of stamped pottery and the use of winter houses and blowguns. In the southern Appalachians, where the Cherokee lived and hunted at the time of white contact in 1542 A.D., there are sites that show signs of continuous use dating back to 9000 B.C. These include hunting camps high in the mountains and villages like the one on Williams Island near present-day Chattanooga, Tennessee. Archaeologists cannot say that these people were not Cherokee. Moreover, linguistic evidence suggests that the Cherokee language began to show unique characteristics at least 3,500 years ago. And since all cultures tell stories, we must assume that these people, living in the southern Appalachians in villages along the rivers and hunting camps on the mountaintops near the balds, did the same.

➤➤ Storytelling Events

Today, stories are told by Cherokee people at home and in public, and more are known and told than will ever be recorded. In the town of Cherokee, North Carolina, stories are told in the schools, at the Cherokee Museum, at the Oconaluftee Living History Village, at the Tsali Manor retirement home, and at various events during the year, including a monthly meeting of elders at Robert Bushyhead's home. Although children may not live in extended families as often as they did in the past, they are hearing more traditional Cherokee stories in school.

Throughout the year, classes about Cherokee language and culture are available. In the spring, storytellers visit the schools to share stories during Cultural Heritage Week. During the Fall Festival, held the first week in October, Cherokee culture is celebrated in many ways. Outside of the Cherokee community, Cherokee storytellers and craftspeople appear at regional festivals like Mountain Heritage Day at Western Carolina University in Cullowhee, at the Giduwah Festival in Asheville, and at powwows throughout the region.

Stories in this book were collected during storytelling events both inside and outside the Cherokee community. I heard Kathi Littlejohn tell stories at the Cherokee Elementary School and Freeman Owle speak publicly in Franklin, North Carolina, in a performance sponsored by the Nantahala Hiking Club. Edna Chekelelee performed on a "Sisters of the South" tour sponsored by the Southern Arts Federation, and Kathi and Edna addressed the Cherokee Speakers' Bureau (Kekasuyeta) about stories. I also conducted personal interviews with each of the storytellers. These and other storytellers now travel the country sharing Cherokee history and stories with executives, doctors, schoolteachers, other American Indians, and the wider public in settings that range from concert halls to living rooms to reenactors' rendezvous.

In traditional Cherokee culture, as in other cultures with living traditions of storytelling, stories are often sprinkled throughout conversation, embedded in the flow of events and casual talk. They make a point or teach a lesson relevant to the events or the conversation in progress. For example, if a child starts bragging, at some time either then or maybe later that day the story about the possum's losing his tail will come up—told in a way that doesn't embarrass the child with a direct rebuke, but in a way that makes the child understand that the moral of the story is meant to apply to him or her. These private storytellings occur frequently and are just as important, in terms of collecting and understanding stories, as public events.

Public storytellings take place when storytellers visit schools or lecture halls and speak to an audience that might or might not be from the storyteller's own culture. Because this book is intended for a general audience, it focuses on public events featuring well-known storytellers. In the past several hundred years, authors and anthropologists have at times sought out "Indian secrets" in order to titillate audiences and make money. In contrast, this collection is solidly based on information that Cherokee storytellers either have already made public or have chosen to make public through this book.

The first time I heard a traditional Cherokee story, I was riding with Hawk Littlejohn in his pickup truck. We had met at the Smithsonian Institution, and I had come to visit him and his family in Murphy, North Carolina, in 1980. Hawk and I were on our way to the feed store and had been chatting about our past experiences with people. I had just recounted some of my problems with relationships when Hawk lit a cigarette, blew out the smoke into the cab of the truck, and said, "You know, once there was an old man crossing over Soco Gap.

"That's going east from Cherokee towards Maggie Valley. And it was the fall of the year, and it was cold. And just as he got over the top of the gap, and was starting down, he looked down and saw a rattlesnake laying there beside the trail. And it was frozen, about froze to death. And because he was ani-yunwiya, one of the real people, he had compassion on his relative. And he reached down and picked up that rattlesnake and put it inside his shirt to warm it up. Well, he was coming down the mountain, and he felt the snake move a little bit. And he came down a little further, and the snake moved a little more. Come on down the mountain, and the air was getting warmer, and the snake was moving around. Come on down a little more, and the snake was moving around, and it bit him. And he reached inside his shirt and pulled the snake out and said, 'Why'd you bite me? I picked you up and saved your life, and now you've bit me and I might die!' And the snake said, 'You knew I was a rattlesnake when you picked me up.'"

I sat there for a minute taking this in. "You knew I was a rattlesnake when you picked me up," Hawk repeated.

"Uh huh," I said, "and this means?"

"If you know somebody's a rattlesnake," he said, "you don't have to pick them up." And I learned a story and a lesson.

>> Stories in Cherokee, Stories in English

The stories that James Mooney collected from the Cherokee more than a century ago were told in the Cherokee language. Today these stories are told publicly in English, although in some families they are still told in Cherokee. Why is this? Has the change in languages changed the stories themselves?

Mooney was "salvaging" cultural materials. His employer and publisher, the U.S. Bureau of Ethnology, had sent its staff to actively collect American Indian materials throughout the country because it knew that other agencies in the federal government were trying to acculturate American Indians* as rapidly as possible and, in the process, eradicate much of their traditional culture.

In the late 1800s, all Cherokee in western North Carolina spoke Cherokee, and many of them read and wrote it as well, thanks to the adoption of Sequoyah's syllabary in the 1820s. About one in four Cherokee spoke some English, and some were also fluent in reading and writing it. But beginning in 1884 and continuing into the late twentieth century, the federal government actually prohibited the speaking of native languages in government-run schools. As a result, only about a thousand members (one in ten) or fewer of the Eastern Band now speak Cherokee as their first language. In recent years, however, interest in all aspects of traditional culture, including language and storytelling, has blossomed. Since the Eastern Band took over the administration of its schools—two elementary schools and a junior/senior high school—from the Bureau of Indian Affairs in 1990, Cherokee language and culture have been taught in the schools for the first time. Children are learning to speak and write Cherokee in classes, and adults are speaking it more at home, often in response to their children's enthusiasm.

To tell the stories in English is to change them somewhat, simply because Cherokee and English are different in many ways. The Cherokee language is centered on verb stems that may have as many as four prefixes and four suffixes. Some prefixes and suffixes are determined by the speaker's relationship to the one addressed, by the direction in which the speaker is facing—east, south, west, or north—or by the inanimate or animate nature of direct objects. Because these concerns are not reflected in the English language, the stories come out somewhat differently. Also, Cherokee speech is full of puns. Humorous comparisons occur when an accent or an inflec-

---

*The Eastern Cherokee prefer the term "American Indian" to "Native American." Their legal name is "the Eastern Band of Cherokee Indians." In informal conversation they refer to themselves as "Indians" and to the Cherokee language as "Indian language."

tion is changed, altering the meaning of a word, and of course this play on words does not translate into English.

Still, the English versions are full of meaning and memorable characters and events. Most important, they have become traditional tellings in themselves as English-speaking parents and elders pass them on to younger generations.

➤➤ Eastern and Western Cherokee Stories

The Eastern Band of Cherokee Indians in western North Carolina and the Cherokee Nation in Oklahoma share language, culture, history, and stories. Among the western Cherokee, stories, medicine formulas, and other folklore have been extensively collected (Jack and Anna Kilpatrick have been particularly active collectors), and storytelling there continues to be very much alive. Although Eastern and Western Cherokee came from the same ancestors less than two hundred years ago, the geographical separation has brought about some differences in both language and storytelling.

The Western Cherokee language, a dialect separate from Eastern Cherokee, originated in the Overhill dialect spoken by the Cherokee living in east Tennessee, north Georgia, and the far western parts of North Carolina such as present-day Graham County, where this dialect is still spoken. Eastern Cherokee is the Kituwah dialect, which originated in what James Mooney described as the Middle dialect spoken in the "Middle towns" along the Oconaluftee and Little Tennessee Rivers in western North Carolina, where the ancestors of today's Eastern Band lived. The separation of more than 150 years has amplified the differences in the two dialects, but even today Eastern and Western Cherokee people easily understand each other and use the same Cherokee syllabary.

Like the language, the stories have remained essentially the same. The Western Cherokee storytelling tradition has added tales from the turbulent period following Removal, such as those about the legendary "outlaw" Ned Christie. The Eastern tradition has retained more place names in stories, because those places are nearby and familiar to the storytellers and their audiences, though they have lost significance for the Western Cherokee.

›› **Genres**

Folklorists have distinguished among genres for their own purposes in understanding and talking with each other about stories. We consider a "legend" to be a story about a historical person or place that is told as though it is true; legends may take the form of scattered comments rather than a coherent narrative. A "myth" is a narrative that explains large philosophical questions of life and death and origins. A "folktale" is a narrative about a person or animal character who goes through a series of events, often a quest. A "fable" is a short animal story with a clear moral, like Aesop's fables. A "parable" or "allegory" is a narrative with symbolic parallels and meanings for every aspect of the story, such as Pilgrim's Progress by John Bunyan or the New Testament parables told by Jesus.

Folklorists also recognize, however, that cultures construct their own classifications of their stories, based on what is important to them. Among the Cherokee, the word "legend" is often used to describe any traditional story, perhaps due to the influence of Mary Chiltoskey, the white schoolteacher who collected many stories and referred to them all as legends, meaning old stories told as if they were true. Edna Chekelelee, however, once told me that there are four kinds of Cherokee stories: happy stories, sad stories, bad stories, and legends. The happy stories include all kinds of animal stories and folktales. Sad stories are about events with unhappy endings, and these include accounts of the Trail of Tears. Bad stories are about people who did things that were considered to be bad, like abandoning children. Legends, or "legend stories," are about things that happened very long ago, including myths and stories of strange supernatural events.

›› **The Stories Themselves**

The stories collected here include all of the above genres, or kinds of stories: myths, legends, folktales, fables, and at least one allegory. They are the stories that the storytellers wanted to tell for this book.

Also included are what folklorists call "personal experience narratives" and "oral history." Davey Arch's stories about his grandfather's experiences as a young boy are tales that Davey was told and will probably tell his children and grandchildren—and they are traditional, too. People of all cultures will recognize stories like this from their own family experiences. Folklorists consider such stories traditional because they are told over and over again in the same form, shaped by the artistry of the teller and the aesthetic of the tradition. Like all stories, they are reshaped a little bit each time they are told, but they remain essentially the same, just as cornbread turns out a little different every time, even though you use the same recipe. Although stories of this type are specific to one person's life or family, they are recognized by other Cherokee as part of a genre that is shared by many people. For example, many older Cherokee people's accounts of their boarding school experiences mirror the experiences and stories of Robert Bushyhead.

Although they are unique to each individual, personal-experience narratives are told in a stylized fashion, with a rhythm different from everyday speech. Telling them in a memorable and entertaining way—an audience is needed, after all, to make this a story—requires as much artistry as relating a possum story or complex myth. Freeman Owle's story about what happened to his great-great-grandfather on the Trail of Tears is both a personal-experience story, a family tradition, and also what scholars call "oral history," the recounting of personal events that are part of a larger historical event. Five hundred years ago Cherokee people were probably telling stories about their grandparents and about "recent" historical events. Particular stories and particular kinds of stories last because we need them in order to learn how to live our lives in the present.

Cherokee stories are shaped by Cherokee culture, including its values and aesthetics and its southern Appalachian environment. Like other American Indian stories, these tend to group events and details in fours or sevens, rather than in the threes common in European folktales. This pattern occurs because the numbers four and seven are sacred to the Cherokee, as they are to many other American Indians. Four is sacred because of the four cardinal directions, east, south, west, and north, each of which is associated with a color and other particular qualities. Seven is sacred because it adds the directions of sky and earth and "the center" to the four cardinal directions. There are seven Cherokee clans, for example. In the rhythm of the stories, phrases, incidents, and details tend to fall into groups of fours as well. There are no princesses in these tales because the Cherokee did not have princesses.

Readers will notice that different versions of the same story, told by different storytellers, are included. This duplication shows that some stories are especially popular and also allows the reader to make comparisons. "The Origin of Strawberries," told by both Freeman Owle and Davey Arch, is told by Kathi Littlejohn as "First Man and First Woman." "How the Possum Lost His Tail" is also told by all three of these storytellers. "The Ball Game of the Birds and Animals" is told by both Kathi Littlejohn and Freeman Owle. Looking at the different versions, you can see how individual storytellers use details and dialogue in unique ways, and you can see how a story can be at once very different and yet the same. These are great stories, and people love to tell them and hear them. They share some of the lessons considered most important in Cherokee culture: getting along with people without getting angry and acting impulsively; refraining from bragging; and remembering that everyone, no matter how different, has an important role to play.

Living Stories of the Cherokee is intended not to provide extensive analysis of Cherokee stories and culture, but to document and celebrate the stories and their sound. Because it is the first major collection of Eastern Band stories in a hundred years, I hope it will be useful to scholars of Native American studies and Cherokee studies, to anthropologists and folklorists. The book also provides materials useful to scholars interested in the role of women in Cherokee culture, the place of storytelling in culture, and a host of other specific topics such as medicine or clan relationships. The index is designed to quickly guide the reader to specific topics of interest.

➤➤ What Makes a Storyteller?

It is the process of learning stories in a traditional setting, from family and community, that makes a storyteller "traditional." Some of the storytellers represented here occasionally take stories from the pages of James Mooney's collection and other printed sources, but all have grown up in a storytelling tradition and learned how to tell stories from parents, grandparents, and the Cherokee community—

at home, at family gatherings, at work, and in the course of daily life. To a folklorist, this makes them traditional Cherokee storytellers. In these situations, much information beyond just the story is imparted, including the values of the culture, its aesthetic, and its style of telling—timing, emphasis, inflection. None of these can be learned, by even the most skilled nontraditional storyteller, from reading a story in a book.

Cherokee stories are still being told, in English and Cherokee, in these traditional settings. Dozens of older women and men tell their stories to the children who come to visit them in the afternoons at the Tsali Manor retirement home in Cherokee; grandfathers and grandmothers tell stories to their grandchildren; and the children themselves, who are learning these stories, tell them to their friends and, perhaps one day, will tell them to their own children.

›› Oral Poetics and Transcription

The stories in this collection are presented on the page as free verse because that style best represents how they are told. They are transcribed directly from the storytellers' words. The storytellers all speak in a rhythmic style that becomes obvious as soon as one starts to write down the words. I have not changed any of the words to make these stories more "literary" or to force them into "standard" English. Punctuation and capitalization follow regular English usage in order to help readers follow the story. The storytellers, like most of us, occasionally speak in sentence fragments. The stories are arranged in lines that represent the natural breaks in the storytellers' speech. If you will read them aloud, or at least listen to them in your mind, you will hear the voices of the storytellers.

This method of transcribing stories from traditional cultures is called "oral poetics," and it was first used by Dennis Tedlock and others in the 1970s. When I studied folklore and the ethnography of speaking with Dell Hymes at the University of Pennsylvania in the 1970s, Hymes was using this format to record the Native American tales he was collecting and studying. Henry Glassie presented stories from Northern Ireland in the same way in *Passing the Time in Ballymenone* and *Irish Folk Tales*.

Using the oral poetics method, one writes down stories word for word directly as spoken by the storytellers. The editor does not add any words at all, for explanation or transition or any other purpose. Stories are broken into lines determined by pauses for breath, because the storyteller's breathing helps to organize his or her thoughts.

When we speak to each other in normal conversation we use words, but we also use timing, inflection, body language, gestures, tone of voice, and eye contact to convey meaning. Some linguists have speculated that these physical aspects of speech convey as much as 85 percent of our meaning, and these are lost when speech is written down. Many of the conventions of standard English serve to clarify meanings that are readily apparent in verbal communication. For example, in conversation we easily follow who is meant by "she" or "them," whereas in written English a number of rules are needed to govern pronoun reference to make certain the reader understands that which, in conversation, is conveyed by a pause or the lift of an eyebrow.

When our everyday conversations are taped and transcribed, they may seem like nonsense on the printed page, and at best they are somewhat ungrammatical. Only the most practiced speakers and lecturers speak in anything resembling standard English, and they have made a great effort to do so. The rest of us speak in dialects influenced by our cultural backgrounds (Cherokee, German American, African American), by our geographical areas of origin (southern Appalachia, the Midwest, Boston), and by our audiences (we speak differently to our children, our bosses, and our friends). No matter how expertly we write standard English, we use linguistic dialects when we speak, because speaking and writing are different media that have different capabilities and serve different purposes.

Using the oral poetics method to transcribe stories from oral tradition enables us to hear the storyteller's words and rhythms and also to understand the storyteller's meaning without changing his or her words. Whereas novelists can present realistic conversation by the use of surrounding narrative and descriptive phrases, the oral poetics method uses the lines and spaces that form the conventions of poetry. This process is made feasible because most storytellers' language is different from that of normal conversation; it is more elegant, rhythmic, and evocative—like poetry.

Stories are presented in lines, the length of which is determined by the storyteller's pauses, which may be for breath or for emphasis. When the storyteller wants to convey excitement, the rhythm of the story gets quicker, and this appears on the page as shorter lines with more frequent breaks. When a storyteller wants to emphasize the main idea, his or her tone of voice conveys this. On the page, it appears as a line that begins at the lefthand margin of the page; it is usually the beginning of a sentence, also. Ideas and phrases given less emphasis by the storyteller's inflection and tone of voice appear on the page indented to the right. Sometimes phrases with even less emphasis are indented even further right, especially if they are dependent clauses. Thus the placement of lines on the page and the length of lines represent both the sound of the storyteller's voice and the meaning of his or her words. A reader who was not present at the actual storytelling event can, to some extent, experience the storyteller's voice by reading the lines aloud.

Oral poetics helps us understand that the language of storytelling is different from the language of everyday life. Its rhythms and repetitions help listeners to enter the world of the story; they also help the storyteller to remember the story. The language used by storytellers reflects their cultures' aesthetics—those things that a culture finds beautiful and "right." And a culture's aesthetics reflects its worldview, so that in the language of storytellers we find the distilled beliefs of a group—in this case the Cherokee—based on many years of experience living together in the southern Appalachians. All this is encoded not only in the content of the words, but in the way they are used by traditional storytellers.

Henry Glassie gave me the following good advice: "The old people talk, you run the machine, you present the tales as accurately and elegantly as you are able. Get them down for the future. The People don't want our analysis. Analysis is ephemeral. Text is permanent. Just follow your heart and do what needs to be done."

>> Stories and Worldview

Stories provide a way for both outsiders and insiders to understand and to remember the larger worldview of the culture, since stories reflect this worldview while also reinforcing it. Anthropologists, sociologists, popularizers, and others have written many books and papers on the subject of the Cherokee worldview, but it is still not fully understood by either scholars or the public. When a woman asked Freeman Owle, after a storytelling performance, what she could read to understand "the mind" of the Cherokee, he suggested reading James Mooney's *Myths and Sacred Formulas of the Cherokee* and Forrest Carter's *The Education of Little Tree*. He also suggested sitting in the woods and listening to the wind. An understanding of the Cherokee worldview (or any worldview) has to be experiential as well as intellectual.

The Cherokee believe that stories, along with ceremonies, arts and crafts, and other traditions, help the individual and the culture to "stay in balance." The Cherokee attribute their survival as a people, a unique culture, to their closeness to the land and their adherence to *Duyukta*. Duyukta is a moral code that might be roughly translated as "the right way," "the right path," or "the path of being in balance."

One of the medicine people told me: "What does being in balance mean? It is the traditional Cherokee way of living: placing importance on the good of the whole more than the individual; having freedom but taking responsibility for yourself; staying close to the earth and all our relations. And how does one do this? By taking time to dream; by understanding our nature and our needs and taking care of them; by doing ceremonies that keep us in balance like going to water and using the sweat lodge; by listening and praying; by recognizing our dark and light sides; by having the support of family, extended family, clan and tribe. The medicine people say it requires understanding ourselves and our place in the world around us."

A new, permanent exhibit at the Museum of the Cherokee Indian in Cherokee, North Carolina, uses these two concepts—the land and Duyukta—as organizing principles. The traditional Cherokee wampum belt is also used in the exhibit as a graphic symbol because of a story told by Lloyd Sequoyah in 1978. While providing information in the case between the Eastern Band and the Tennessee Valley Authority, in which the Eastern Band challenged the TVA's plan to flood the old capital city of Echota in Tennessee for the Tellico Dam project (the suit was unsuccessful and the city was flooded), Lloyd Sequoyah told attorneys:

Years ago,
>during the time when the whites were coming into this country,
>things were hard for the Cherokee.

One day, an old man came to the city of Old Echota,
>and he called all the people into the townhouse to hear him
>>speak.

Before he spoke he took a wampum belt
>and threw it up over two of the crossbeams
>between the posts that held up the seven-sided council house.

He told the people that times were hard for them,
>and that they would get harder.

But they would survive as a people, he said,
>if they would follow the traditional way of the Cherokee people:
>Duyukta, the path of harmony, of being in balance.

They asked him what the wampum belt meant, and he explained.

The man and woman on one end of the belt represent the Cherokee
>>people.

The white path of beads down the center of the belt
>represents Duyukta, the path of harmony, of being in balance.

The black beads on both sides of the white path
>represent all the things that you can do
>to stray from the path of being in harmony.

The checkerboard of squares at the other end of the belt
>represents all the good things that will come to you
>at the end of life's journey
>if you stay on the path of harmony.

He said that
>as long as the Cherokee people stayed on the path of harmony
>>and balance,
>and the wampum belt survived,
>that the Cherokee would survive as a people.

As he finished speaking the wampum belt burst into flame.

The people were horrified,
>thinking this signified the end of them as a people.

But when the flames died down,
>they saw that the belt was still intact:
>all of the beads, threads, and deerskin backing.

And they knew they would survive as a people
    if they would follow the path of harmony and balance.

Lloyd Sequoyah believed that this wampum belt had been lost in the Removal in 1838. Several years after his testimony, however, anthropologist Duane King found that this same belt was being kept by the Cherokee Kituwah Society in Oklahoma.

As the Cherokee people begin the twenty-first century, they continue to try to stay in balance, recognizing that "life is change. Whether you think things are good or bad, they're going to change." Casino gambling has been introduced on the Qualla Boundary. Growth and development have created an urgent need for housing. At the same time, children are learning the Cherokee language in school for the first time ever. Important archaeological sites are being cataloged and preserved. More traditional storytellers than ever are sharing Cherokee stories in public. And for the first time in more than a hundred years, the Eastern Cherokee have made a major purchase to reclaim some of their ancestral homeland: the nearby tract of three hundred acres that includes the ancient Kituwah Mound, the site of the first Cherokee village in the long-ago time of stories, when people and animals could talk to each other. And at the ceremony dedicating the Kituwah Mound and village site, there were speeches, recognition of elders, prayers, "Amazing Grace" sung in Cherokee by a children's chorus, and, of course, stories. Jerry Wolf told the story of Tsali with tears in his voice. "When I put my head on my pillow at night, I think of Tsali sleeping with his head on a rock so that we could be here today." Stories of ancient prophecies and migrations. Stories of families removed and returned. The stories, the land, the balance, the Cherokee people continue. This book is dedicated to that process.

>> Kathi Smith Littlejohn

Kathi Littlejohn was born in Cherokee in the 1950s and graduated from high school there. In her early years, her parents taught school in Michigan, Florida, and Oklahoma. Today Kathi works as Health and Human Services Director for the tribe and tells stories mainly in the schools. She has produced two cassette tapes of her stories and has become well known for her dramatic, entertaining style.

Kathi went to community college at night and took education classes part-time for thirteen years until she graduated from Western Carolina University in 1986. When assigned, in a children's literature class, to present a story to the class, she chose a Cherokee legend. After the other teachers heard it, they asked Kathi to come to their schools and tell Cherokee stories. She thought that was really fun: "And so I started learning more and telling the ones I already knew."

Although Kathi did not hear many legends from her parents when she was growing up, she did learn them from other members of the Cherokee community. When she was fourteen, she was a guide at the Oconaluftee Indian Village and Living History Museum. On days when the weather was bad and few tour groups came through, the older workers would sit and talk, telling traditional stories to the younger Cherokee tour guides. "But I never dreamed of telling them again until I started in that class," Kathi said.

Now Kathi has four stepchildren and a young child of her own, and she shares her stories with them. Her teenagers have been involved both in producing Kathi's tapes of legends and in film productions of legends in their school. Her nineteen-month-old baby is still just amazed at the sound of his mother's voice coming from a stereo speaker.

Kathi, like others, has seen a lot of recent interest in storytelling. As late as the 1980s, no one but Mary Chiltoskey was telling legends in public. Kathi explained, "Of course people told them in their homes, but there were no school projects like there are today. And since then more people have started telling them. We have Carl Lloyd Owle, we have Freeman Owle and Lloyd Arneach, and of course Davey Arch and Fred Bradley. And lots of people now are starting to tell the legends that they know."

She sees the greatest growth, however, in school projects. Students have written plays based on Cherokee legends, and some of these have been performed in the preshow for Unto These Hills, the outdoor drama in Cherokee. Classes in the schools have produced plays, puppet shows, videos, and giant books with illustrations. "So there's just a real interest and a real steady growth and expansion of ideas on the legends."

In fact, there is a growing appreciation for and use of all aspects of traditional culture—not just legends—in the schools. Students wear t-shirts that say "I'm drug free" in the Cherokee language, with designs using the turtle and the spider from Cherokee stories.

Students take Cherokee language classes and also learn traditional arts and crafts. According to Kathi, "One little kindergarten girl said, 'My grandma makes pottery and I do, too.' " Kathi, along with many others, gives credit to Chief Joyce Dugan, who has supported cultural activities and has formed a cultural heritage department for the tribe. As part of a special grant to combat substance abuse, a dance class is offered on the tribe's ceremonial grounds. Walker Calhoun, a respected elder who has received the National Endowment for the Arts Folk Heritage Award (in 1993), the North Carolina Folk Heritage Award, and the Sequoyah Award, teaches Cherokee traditional dancing.

Like many others of her generation, Kathi was raised to speak English, even though her grandparents were fluent speakers of Cherokee. She now encourages her mother-in-law and father-in-law to speak Cherokee to her children at home. "The language just wasn't taught in the schools when I was going to school, and it wasn't taught at home." Kathi confirms that many, if not all, Cherokee families continue to tell stories in their homes—legends, family stories, and oral histories—both in English and in Cherokee.

Kathi is always learning new stories from older members of the community, from children in her audiences, and from her own research. Her husband's family still tells a story about the Removal, and her husband's great-aunt is a direct descendant of Tsali; Kathi wants to collect their stories. She would like to see a legend archive created, she would like to start a Native American storytelling festival, and she would like to work with groups of students to produce plays and videos. Every year, just before the Cherokee fall festival, young girls seek out Kathi to learn legends to perform in the "traditional talent" category of the Little Miss Cherokee pageant. Her eyes light up when she says, "I would love to take a group of young people and work with them on not just writing it down or doing it as a classroom project but for them to BE the legend tellers, you know, and work with them like that."

Kathi's storytelling style is dramatic and entertaining, with lots of dialogue, expressive voices, and questions to engage her mostly young audiences. When I ask Kathi where she got her storytelling style, she credits her mother. "She's just real enthusiastic. She is such a cheerleader, and she's always been such a motivator for any of us." But the most intriguing explanation of Kathi's style comes from another storyteller, Carl Lloyd Owle. "You know," he said, "Kathi, I believe when you tell legends, angels sit on your shoulders."

»

Kathi's stories in this book were collected in two sessions at the Cherokee Elementary School, during Cultural Heritage Week in 1995 and 1996, and from her two cassette tapes. Of the sixteen stories included here, half are animal tales like "How the Possum Lost His Beautiful Tail." Kathi tells these stories with a dramatic flair and lots of interesting dialogue between the animals, and her audiences love them. I asked her which ones were the favorites. She replied, "Every year it's still always Spearfinger. They remember the turtle one, more than any of them. And possum. Those are the three requests that I get most often."

Kathi includes in her repertoire the three stories most often told by other Cherokee storytellers: "How the Possum Lost His Tail," "First Man and First Woman" ("The Origin of Strawberries"), and "The Birds and Animals Stickball Game." Of her sixteen stories here, five are not found in James Mooney's collection; seven are variants of stories in Mooney; and four are pretty much like the version in Mooney. The five not found in Mooney at all are "The Origin of Legends," "The Bird with Big Feet," "Me-Li and the Mud Dauber," "The Origin of the Pileated Woodpecker," and "The Valley of the Butterflies." The seven that are different from Mooney's version have significant variations; these are "How the World Was Made," "First Man and First Woman" ("The Origin of Strawberries"), "The Birds and Animals Stickball Game," "The Cherokee Little People," "Nun-nehi, the Gentle People," "Spearfinger," and "How the Possum Lost His Beautiful Tail." Kathi's stories that closely resemble the versions in Mooney are mostly the simpler animal tales: "Why the Turtle's Shell Is Cracked," "The Playing Boys—the Pleiades," "Why the Mole Lives Underground," and "Getting Fire."

›› The Origin of Legends

Today, I'm going to tell you some Cherokee legends.
We were just talking a little bit about what people did a long time
     ago.
They didn't have books did they?
They didn't go to school,
   so they needed legends to teach people
   about different animals
   with stories
   and how things came to be
   and about the rules that everybody was supposed to go by
   so they would treat each other with a lot of respect
   and take care of one another.
That's why we have legends.

››

Why do you think I'm here today?
To tell us legends.

What are legends?
Very good, a tale that was long ago that was true.
But does anybody know how the legends came to be?
How did we get legends?
From your grandfather, very good.
And I'm gonna tell you the first legend
    about how we got legends,
      because at one time there were no grandfathers.
In fact, it was such a long time ago,
    they were young themselves.
A long long long time ago,
    there was a group of people
    that lived by themselves in the world
    with all of the animals.
And they could all talk to one another,
    they could talk to the animals,
    and they had the same language,
    and everybody got along.
And then one day,
    as people will do,
    they started to fight.
One thing led to another,
    and this person wasn't talking to this person.
Another thing happened,
    and this person pushed this person.
Somebody wasn't very nice to somebody,
    and somebody stole something from somebody,
    and they were really really angry at one another.
So angry that they hit each other,
    and they were going to kill one other.
The Creator didn't like this at all.
And so
    he sent them
    —divided them up into groups of four—
    and sent
      one group to the north,
      one to the south,
      one to the east

and one to the west.
All around to the corners of the world.
And once they got there,
 they were very confused,
 because they didn't know how to live
 in this part of the world.
They weren't familiar with these things.
They didn't know where the water was.
They didn't know what kind of plants these were.
They didn't know how to get ready for the winter
 because they didn't know what the winter was gonna be like.
So the Creator felt very sorry for them,
 and he wanted to help them,
 but he wanted them to learn their lesson.
So he sent them a gift.
He sent them dreams
 that told them about each of the animals,
 what to eat,
 what to do,
 what kind of plants they could use for medicine,
 and what kind of plants, if they ate them, would make them sick,
 how to catch that kind of fish,
 how to look at these different kind of animals and use them.
So they began to learn,
 and they began to grow,
 and they began to live in their new home,
 and they got along with each other this time.
Then he sent them another gift
 so they would never forget these things.
He sent them legends,
 about all of these animals
 and all of these plants.
So that each time they told the legend,
 they would remember these animals
 and take better care of them
 and take better care of each other.
And that's how the legends came into the world.
Okay? Now you know? Okay, let's tell another legend.

34

›› The Bird with Big Feet

Have you ever looked in the mirror
    and decided that you wanted to look different?
How would you like to look different?
I wish I was really tall.
I would like to be about six foot tall.
Yeah, I think that would be a good thing.
I would like to be that tall.
I'm five foot five and I would like to be six foot tall.
No, not a giant, I'd just like to be real tall.
I just think that would be a real fun thing to do.
I'd like to be different.
Have you ever looked in the mirror and thought,
    "Gee, I wish I had curly hair,"
    or,
    "Gee I wish I had blonde hair or black hair.
    I wish I looked different."
Do you ever think that?
Well, a long time ago
    there was this bird,
    and this bird was a really nice looking bird,
    except he thought he had too big feet.
Oh, he hated his feet.
He would try to walk through the fields,
    and he'd trip and fall down,
    and all the other animals and the birds would laugh at him.
And they'd say,
    "Well, pick up your feet, and you wouldn't do that."
    "Well, if I had feet that looked like yours I'd stay home."
They said mean things about his feet.
And he was very embarrassed about his feet.
One day, he fell down again.
This time when they laughed at him he thought,
    "I can't stand my feet.
    I'm gonna run away and go live
    where nobody can look at me and my feet ever again."
As he was walking away through the field by himself,

the grasshopper stopped him and said,
　"Where are you going?"
He said,
　"I'm sick and tired of my feet,
　everybody laughs at my feet, they point at my feet, they laugh.
　I'm gonna go live by myself.
　Nobody's gonna have to look at my feet again."
The grasshopper said,
　"I wouldn't be ashamed of that.
　One day your feet will have a very special purpose.
　Don't worry about your feet."
But the bird didn't listen,
　he just stomped on through the grass by himself,
　and he pouted all day.
The next day,
　there were some men that came to cut down the grass in the field
　because they wanted to plant a garden.
What they didn't know was
　that there was a bird's nest,
　with little baby birds in it,
　and if they started cutting down the grass,
　they were probably going to kill the baby birds.
The mother bird heard them talking,
　and she was real upset.
And she tried to fly away
　so that the men would follow her and go away from the nest,
　and they just ignored her.
And then she tried to go and pick up the nest,
　and it was way too heavy,
　and she might drop the eggs,
　and she was just so frantic,
　she didn't know what to do.
The grasshopper saw her and said,
　"You know, I bet you if you go and ask that bird with big feet,
　I bet you he could help you, and help you move your eggs."
So she flew over to the field,
　and she begged him to come and help,
　but he just said,

"Oh not me, I can't help. Why, my big feet!
    What if I fell down and I crushed your babies?"
She said,
    "Oh no, I know you won't, I know you won't.
    Please come and help me. Please."
So he went back with her,
    and she got one egg,
    and put it on one foot,
    and she got the other egg,
    and put it on his other foot,
    because they were
    so big
    that they could hold the egg safely.
She got the other egg,
    and together they moved the baby birds on the other side of the
        field.
The men didn't even see them that day, they were safe.
She was so grateful that he had helped her,
    she was so proud of his big feet,
    she went around and told all the other animals what happened.
And instead of laughing at his feet,
    they just wanted big feet too.
And that's the legend about the bird with big feet.

➤ Me-Li and the Mud Dauber

What's a mud dauber?
And what do mud daubers build?
A house of mud.
They look like little tunnels, don't they?
They're good builders.
A long time ago,
    there was a Cherokee girl by the name of Me-Li.
That's Mary.
And she was just beautiful.
All the boys wanted to talk to her.
Every day she just ignored them.
She wouldn't even look at them.

They would jump in front of her,
    and they'd turn somersaults,
    and they'd try to tickle her and push her,
    anything they could do to get her to look at them.
But she never would.
She just went straight down and did her chores.
She'd every day go down to the river
    and get water and bring it back,
    and she'd have to hurry,
    because all they had a long time ago was
    tightly woven baskets that would carry water,
    and of course they would leak,
    so she'd have to run back as fast as she could
    so all the water wouldn't come out.
And the boys every day
    would try to get her to look at 'em and look at 'em.
Mr. Mud Dauber decided that he really wanted to talk to her,
    and he was gonna get her attention.
He was going to get her to pay attention to him—
    not the boys.
So every day Mr. Mud Dauber would fly around her face—
    th-th-th-th-th-th-th-th-th—
    but she'd just go like that [waves her hand]
    and walk on.
Then he'd try to get around her ears—
    th-th-th-th-th-th-th—
    but she'd just go like that [waves her hand]
    and go on.
And he kept thinking,
    "I'm really, really, really,
    I'm really gonna get you to pay attention to me today."
And every day
    he'd come and zh-zh-zh-zh-zh-zh-zh,
    and she'd ignore him and go on.
Well, this day he decided he would fly down her dress.
He flew down her dress,
    and she stopped
    and screamed

and started going like this [jumping, waving her arms, shaking
    her dress]
trying to get him out.
"Get him out of there,
get out of there go on.
Get out. Fly away."
He was so excited,
    "She's talking to ME!"
And all the other boys saw that,
    and they were so mad
    that the mud dauber got her to stop and talk—
    never mind that she yelled at him—
    but she was paying attention to him,
    and he just loved that.
She was dancin' around
    trying to get the mud dauber out of her dress—
    ze-ze-ze-ze-ze-ze-ze.
She got him out, and she said,
    "You listen to me. Don't you ever do that again!"
Oh, he was just excited,
    "She's really talking to me now."
And she yelled at him all the way down to the creek.
She got so mad that she said,
    "I'll teach you a lesson."
And she went back to his little mud house,
    and she grabbed it off,
    and she threw it in the creek.
And he thought,
    "Ne-ne-ne-ne-na, I'll just make another one."
But she was so mad she stomped off.
And the next day she went back,
    and she saw that that mud was still in the water.
She thought,
    "Well, that's funny.
    How come it didn't fall apart?"
So she picked up the mud, and she looked at it, and she thought,
    "I wonder what would happen if I dried this?"
And see if it would fall apart then.

So she was just playing with it,
    and she kept playing with it for a couple of days,
    and she put it back in the water,
    and she'd take it out, and it got harder and harder.
And she put it in the fire,
    it didn't destroy it, nothing happened.
And she was really surprised about this,
    so she went down to the river and got some mud,
    just like the mud dauber made,
    and she made a little bowl.
And she put it out in the sun
    and let it dry until it got real hard,
    and then she tried to put water in it,
    after she had put it in the fire and made it real hard.
And sure enough
    she could carry more water that way,
    without it leaking like the basket did.
So the mud dauber did a lot more that day than bother Me-Li.
He taught her how to make pottery.
And that's a legend
    about how the Cherokee people got ideas on making pottery,
    from old Mr. Mud Dauber.

❯❯ How the World Was Made

This is another legend about mud.
We like legends about mud.
A long time ago,
    there were only two people and the animals.
And they all lived together
    on a tiny little rock in the middle of the water.
One was a grandfather,
    and one was his grandson, a little baby.
And as babies do,
    he started to grow.
Can you still wear the shoes that you wore when you were in
            kindergarten?
No.

Why?

What happened?

You grew, that's right.

What about, does anybody wear diapers in here?

No.

Because why?

That's just for babies and you got too big, didn't you?

Well, that's what started happening with this baby.

He started growing,

    and he started learning to crawl,

    and then he started learning to walk,

    and then he began to play.

And when he was about your age,

    there was no more room on the rock.

He said,

    "Grandfather, I really wish I had some more room to play.

    I can't do anything, I bump into you, I bump into the animals,

    they bump into me,

    and I'm still growing."

The grandfather thought,

    "You know that is—that's going to be a real problem

    because, what's going to happen when he's sixteen?"

So all the animals started talking about,

    "This is a real problem. What are we going to do?"

So the animals decided that they would dive down into the water

    and try to find some more land.

One tried,

    and went all the way down as far as he could

    and came back and said,

    "I ran out of air. I just can't go any further."

Nobody else wanted to try.

Finally Mr. Turtle said,

    "I can.

    I can stay on the bottom of water for a long time without air.

    Maybe I can find some more land."

So he went down into the water,

    and they all watched him go out of sight,

    and he was gone for seven days.

Finally, on the seventh day,
    they saw some bubbles coming up out of the water,
    and they all ran to look and see if he was coming back.
And slowly they began to see him come into sight,
    and they were very sad
    because he was dead.
The water had killed him.
He'd run out of air and he died.
But then they saw
    that on the bottom of all four of his feet
    there was some mud.
And they carefully got all the mud off,
    and they laid it out on the rock to dry,
    and they watched it carefully.
And when it was dry enough,
    Grandfather threw it out into the water,
    and it became land,
    just as we have land today,
    except it was very soft and very muddy.
And the buzzard flew off of the rock with his great wings,
    and said,
    "With the air from my wings,
    I'll make a fan and dry it
    so we can walk on this new land."
But
    each time when his wings went down,
    it would make a big valley,
    and each time the wings would go up,
    it would make a big mountain.
And pretty soon the animals said,
    "If we don't stop him
    there's not gonna be any land flat enough to walk on."
So they called him back,
    and today,
    when you look all around us,
    what do we have here?
Mountains

where his wings went up and made the mountains,
and valleys
when they went down.
But if they hadn't stopped him,
the whole world would look just like Cherokee.
And that's how the world was made.

›› The Origin of the Pileated Woodpecker

In a Cherokee village
not far from here,
there was an older woman
that was so hateful.
Do you know anybody like that?
I mean hateful.
Like she hated children.
She hated everybody.
But she loved her garden.
Each day
she would dress herself
in a long black skirt
and a red kerchief on the top of her head,
and she would go out and spend hours and hours
among her plants and her trees.
She carefully picked off the bugs,
and she would trim all of the trees each day
and get all of the dead branches and leaves off of them.
She loved her garden.
She was very protective
of all of the plants and trees that lived there,
even to the point where she would scream at the children
if they even got close.
She loved her plants and her flowers, but she didn't like people.
Especially kids that went too close to her garden.
On the other side of her garden was the creek.
That's where everybody went
to throw rocks and go fishing and swim.

Every hot summer day
   the kids would try to go through her garden
   to get down to the creek.
That made her so mad.
She'd run at them,
   and she'd say,
   "Get out of here. I told you to never . . ."
Oh, she'd just scream at them
   something awful
   and scare the kids so bad.
The little ones would cry,
   and the older ones would get mad and say,
   "Well this belongs to everybody.
   You don't have the right to keep us from the swimming hole."
They'd go back and tell their moms and dads,
   and the next day she'd do it again.
   "I said to get out of here.
   Run. I told you, don't you run through here anymore."
Ooh, she was just awful.
But the conjure woman didn't like that
   and thought,
   "You know,
   those kids do have the right to go down to the water."
And she put a spell on her.
And the next time
   that she ran out to her garden and yelled at the kids,
   and she threw up her arms and said,
   "Get away from here,"
   she went up in the air,
   and she kept going,
   and she looked down,
   and her black skirt had turned into black feathers,
   and her red kerchief had turned into a red topknot
   on the top of her head,
   and her arms had turned into wings.
And she turned into a woodpecker.
And even today,
   what do you see a woodpecker do on the trees?

44

Peck and try to get the bugs off of the trees.
And that's the old woman
    trying to get the bugs off of the trees,
    cause she's still trying to take care of her garden.
And that's how we got woodpeckers.

›› The Playing Boys—the Pleiades

Have you ever been playing so hard outside that you didn't want to
        stop?
Even to come in for supper?
Did somebody yell at you and say,
    "You better get in right now"?
Yeah, that happens a lot.
It happened one time with these seven boys.
Every day they would get together,
    and they would play so hard,
    and they loved to dance.
They would dance,
    and they would play,
    and they'd play games,
    and when they were supposed to go do their chores,
    they didn't do 'em.
And when they were supposed to come in for supper,
    they didn't do it,
    and they kept playing the game.
So one day
    their moms said,
    "Let's teach them a lesson.
    When they come in tonight,
    and they're so hungry, and they want their supper,
    let's feed them rocks.
    We'll teach them a lesson.
    We're not gonna give them good food."
So they called them in,
    they never came.
They called them in,
    they never came.

And so finally
    when they came in—
    and it was real dark, and real late, and they were hungry—
    they said,
    "Oh please can we have something to eat?"
They said,
    "You want to eat? Eat these rocks."
And they gave them a big bowl full of rocks.
This made the boys so angry.
They ran out into the middle of the village,
    and they joined hands,
    and they started dancing again.
And they said,
    "We'll just dance all night
    if all you're gonna feed us is rocks."
And they started dancing so fast,
    they started going in a circle,
    and they went so fast that their feet came up off of the ground,
    and they were in the air.
Well, this kind of scared their moms,
    and they were yelling at them to stop dancing.
And they went faster and faster and faster and faster,
    and they got up higher and higher and higher.
So finally
    one of the tallest men reached up and tried to pull them back
        down.
And all he could do was grab one boy,
    and he pulled him so hard
    that he went down into the ground,
    and the earth covered him over.
The other six boys,
    still in a circle,
    went all the way up into the stars.
And even today,
    if you look up there,
    you'll see a group of six stars,
        in a circle,
        still dancing.

Now in English
　　this is called the seven Pleiades, or the Pleiades.
And the seventh boy,
　　that was down in the ground,
　　turned into a pine tree.
And if you'll look at any pine tree,
　　where is the top pointing?
　　Pointing straight up
　　toward the stars where his friends are dancing.
And he's always looking at his friends every night,
　　and he's always green even in the wintertime,
　　so you can see the point,
　　pointing at the circle of boys that are still dancing.

►► **Why the Turtle's Shell Is Cracked**

Now, how many of you know what a turtle looks like?
Are you scared of turtles?
No.
Why?
They're not scary, they don't bark, they don't run fast, do they?
Did you know,
　　that a long time ago,
　　that the turtle was the most ferocious warrior on the face of the
　　　　earth?
He was twenty feet tall.
He was so big and strong,
　　and he was mean,
　　and none of the other animals liked him.
They were all afraid of him, even the wolves.
One day
　　a wolf met the turtle out in the woods,
　　and he thought,
　　"Here comes that mean old turtle.
　I'm not even gonna get out of the way.
　I'm sick and tired of him ordering me around."
But sure enough,
　　the turtle said,

"Get out of my way."
The wolf said,
  "No, no, I was here first."
And the turtle killed him,
    cut off his ears,
    stuck 'em under his belt,
    stepped over the dead body,
    and walked on.
It didn't matter to him.
And he walked all day.
And he was real hungry,
    and he thought,
      "The next time that I come to a village,
      I'm gonna tell them that they have to fix my supper."
And he walked down into the village,
    and it was a wolf village,
    and he said,
      "Hey you, you. You come here and fix me something to eat right
        now."
Well, they were all so scared of him,
    they ran and made him a big bowl of soup,
    and they gave it to him,
    and he pulled out those wolf ears
    and used them as spoons,
    and he ate every bit of that soup,
    he didn't even care that they were wolf ears.
And the other wolves got so upset and mad,
    they said,
      "Look at him.
      He's using the ears of our brother to eat with.
      What is he doing?
      No, not me, I'm scared."
They didn't know what to do.
So they decided that they would hide in the night,
    and the next morning
    all of them would jump on him,
    not just one or two.
So they went out, and they hid,

and the next morning when he woke up,
he thought it was awful funny that nobody was there,
so he began to hurry,
he thought they were gonna trick him.
And he went all the way down to the edge of the river,
and he turned around and here they came:
two hundred snapping snarling wolves,
and they were gonna jump on him.
So he jumped out,
so he could jump into the river and swim away,
but he missed the water,
and he crashed onto the rocks,
and he broke into a hundred pieces.
But, being the mighty warrior that he was,
he sang a magic song,
and the all pieces came together,
and he swam away.
But ever since then
the turtle is very small,
and if you look on his back what do you find?
Cracks.
And that's where
those pieces came together that day.
And that's how come the turtle's shell is cracked.

Why the Mole Lives Underground

Does anybody know what a little mole looks like?
Well, this legend tells us
why the mole lives underground.
Have you ever been in love with anybody?
Anybody have a girlfriend?
Anybody have a boyfriend?
You do?
Well, let me tell you about this young man.
He fell in love with this girl.
Oh, every time he'd see her,
his heart would just go like this:

bump-bump-bump-bump-bump—
    oh, he was so in love with her.
But she wouldn't even look at him.
Oh, he'd follow her around,
    and he'd bring her flowers
    and try to talk to her.
She wouldn't even look at him.
Oh, he was just sick.
He wanted to marry her.
Yeah, and she wouldn't even talk to him.
So he went,
    and he asked all of the conjure people
    if they would put a spell on her
    and make her fall in love with him.
And they couldn't do it.
So the little mole said,
    "I can help you."
And he said,
    "You?
    You're so tiny, what can you do?"
"You watch."
And that night
    he snuck into her room while she was asleep,
    and he went down,
    and he stole her heart.
And he brought it to the young man,
    and he said,
    "Now you have her heart.
    She will love only you."
And the next morning
    the girl woke up and said,
    "You know, I've been having the strangest dreams all night."
And went to see the boy
    and said,
    "I dreamed that I gave you my heart,
    and I think I love you."
Oh, he was so excited,
    and he said,

"Will you marry me?"
And she said,
　"Yes."
But the conjure men were so mad at that mole
　　because he had stronger magic than they did,
　　and they were gonna murder him,
　　they were gonna kill the mole.
And they ran and tried to catch him,
　　and the only place he could go
　　was down under the ground.
And you know,
　　even today
　　he's scared to come out,
　　because they might still be trying to kill him.
And that's why the mole lives under the ground.

How the Possum Lost His Beautiful Tail

Let's hear another one.
Anybody want to hear another one?
What does a possum look like?
Do you think possums are very pretty?
Possums are not very pretty animals if you ask me,
　　but did you know
　　a long time ago
　　that the possum had the most beautiful tail
　　of all the animals?
It was long and thick and beautiful,
　　and he was so proud of that tail.
Did you know that he was so proud of that tail
　　that all he did was comb his tail?
He'd comb it,
　　and he'd braid it,
　　and he'd put ribbons in it,
　　and the other animals didn't like that.
They'd say,
　　"Possum, come and help me today."
And he'd say,

"Oh no. I've got to wash my tail."
And they'd say,
    "Well possum, how are you today?"
And he'd swish around,
    and he'd stick that old tail in their face
    and say,
    "Me and my tail are just fine, thank you very much."
Well, they didn't like that.
It wasn't nice.
And so
    the possum was so conceited and thinking about his tail,
    he never once thought that the fox had a pretty tail,
    that other animals had pretty tails.
    He didn't care.
But they decided that they were gonna get rid of his tail.
And they knew
    that he had wanted to be the lead dancer,
    so they wouldn't let him
    'cause his tail would get in the way.
But this time
    they said,
    "You can be the lead dancer."
And sure enough
    he was so excited
    he went over to the cricket,
    and he said, "I want you to fix my tail."
'Cause cricket was the barber to all the animals.
And he combed his hair,
    and he hummed a little song,
    until possum fell asleep.
And when he fell asleep,
    cricket cut off every hair on his tail,
    made it so ugly and naked.
Eogh.
Then to hide it,
    he tied it up in a ribbon,
    and when possum saw that he said,
    "What have you done?"

He said,

"Oh, I have made a beautiful tail hair design.
Don't take the ribbon off until you're dancing.
Then everyone will love it."

Well, possum was there the next morning,
and they started,
and he was the lead dancer,
and he stepped out and started dancing,
and he reached back and took that ribbon off,
and sure enough
everybody pointed at his tail.

Oh, he loved it,
he danced so hard,
he'd throw that old tail around,
and then,
he saw that
they were laughing and pointing at his tail,
and he thought,
"Laughing? They aren't supposed to laugh at my tail."

And he looked back over his shoulder,
and he saw that naked, bony-looking tail.

He was so embarrassed, guess what he did?
He rolled over and played like he was dead.
And even today,
that's what possums will do,
they'll roll over and play like they're dead.

And that is how the possum lost his beautiful,
beautiful tail.

▶ Getting Fire

A long time ago,
they didn't have fire
on our side of the world,
and everything was real dark and real cold.

They knew
that there was fire on the other side of the world,
and all the animals wanted some fire.

So one by one
   they said that they were gonna go get the fire.
First,
   the buzzard went.
And he flew way around
   on the other side of the world,
   and he saw some of the fire,
   and he tried to get some.
And he got a real coal,
   a real hot coal,
   and he thought,
   "Great, I got some.
   And I'm gonna fly back
   and take it back on the other side of the world."
And he put it right on top of his head
   and flew off.
And what happened?
It burned off all the feathers on the top of his head.
Oh, it was so hot
   he went and stuck his head in the lake.
And no fire.
Everybody tried.
Finally
   the little black snake went all the way around on the other side of
      the world,
   (but the snake wasn't even black then).
He stole from the fire.
He didn't have a good place to carry it,
   so he put on the back of his neck,
   and it burnt him black all the way down.
And he's still black.
So he got into the lake to put the fire out.
So he didn't get fire either.
Now they didn't know what to do.
Finally,
   Grandmother Spider said,
   "I may be small,
   but I'm gonna go get the fire."

"You!"
　　all the other animals laughed.
"You can't even make it,
　　you're so small
　　you can't carry that fire."
She said,
　　"I might be small, but I'll go get the fire.
　　You watch me."
She went all the way on the other side of the world,
　　but this time she was thinking,
　　"Now, those other animals tried to steal it,
　　and it was too hot,
　　so I need to put it in something.
　　Hmmmm. What can I put it in?"
She went down to the river,
　　she made a little pot of clay,
　　and she put it on her back.
When she went and got some of the coals,
　　the hot coals,
　　she put it right in the pot.
She made it all the way back
　　and gave everybody some fire.
But then she also gave the Cherokee people
　　the idea of making pottery.

>> First Man and First Woman

Now,
　　how many of you have ever had a fight
　　with your brother or sister,
　　your best friend or teacher?
Oh no, no, now you better not tell me you had a fight with your
　　　　　teacher.
Oh my goodness.
Did—
　　before you know it—
　　you were yelling ugly mean things
　　that you really didn't mean to say,

mainly about what they looked like and smelled like,
they were kind of stupid,
and you hated them,
and you really didn't,
but when we get angry
we say these things without thinking first, don't we.
Well, a long time ago,
    that's exactly what happened between first man and first woman.
And they were so much in love,
    and they loved one another,
    and they loved their animal friends.
What happened that day
    nobody can even remember,
    but all of a sudden first woman said,
    "You are the slowest man on the face of the earth.
    I asked you two days ago to help me with this,
    and now look what happened."
        "Well, you call me slow, you're as slow as an old turtle."
    "I asked you if you'd do this."
    "And not only that, but you're fat."
    "Fat, well you're ugly."
Oh, the ugly things they said about one another,
    and oh, he got so mad,
    and they were yelling and screaming.
First woman burst into tears,
    and she ran out the door.
He ran after her,
    and he hollered,
    "You go on and don't you ever come back."
Oh, and he was still so angry,
    and he stomped around,
    and he thought,
    "She called me fat! Fat? How dare she?
    She ought to look at herself before she—
    Oh, don't you ever come back and tell me that."
Then it got later and later,
    and he got a little more worried about her.
So he went to the edge of the clearing and kinda called her name,

and no answer.
And he thought,
   "That's all right.
   You stay out there all night.
   See if I care."
And he walked back in and slammed the door,
   and it got real late, and real dark.
There were no lights then,
   and he was really worried, and he thought,
   "Gosh, what if something really has happened to her?
   Oh no, oh I can't wait to see her and tell her I'm sorry.
   I told her she was ugly. She's not ugly.
   Oh, I'm so sorry."
And at first light, the next day,
   he started out to try to find where she was,
   and he began to see little signs,
   and he found a broken leaf or a broken branch,
   and he could see the bent grass where she ran.
So pretty soon,
   he started noticing that there was a little flower,
   just about the space of a woman's foot if she was running,
   and it was in a straight line.
He'd never seen these flowers before,
   and he followed the little white flowers
   that led him straight to where she was.
She had lain down and gone to sleep.
She stayed right there so he could find her.
He woke her up and said,
   "Oh, my baby, I'm so sorry."
And she went,
   "Oh, smooch smooch honey darlin'."
Oh, mushy mushy.
And they promised they wouldn't fight any more,
   they put their arms around each other,
   and started walking back home, lovey-dovey.
And as they stepped over each of the white flowers,
   they bloomed out into a strawberry.
And the strawberries are supposed to remind us now

not to ever fight with the people that we care about.
They're just a reminder
   about the first man and first woman's fight,
   and how we got strawberries in the world.

That's how the Cherokee people got the first strawberries.
And the legend goes on to tell us
   that we should keep them in our home at all times:
      maybe a picture,
      maybe jelly,
      it may be strawberry jam.
To remind us not to argue
   as first man and first woman did.

›› The Valley of the Butterflies

Now, how 'bout another love story.
How many of you have got a boyfriend?
How many of you have got a girlfriend?
Uh-huh.
One brave fella tells the truth.
There was a young woman, about your age, and she was bored.
She was bored with her life.
She thought her family was stupid,
   she thought her work and her chores were stupid,
     same old same old.
Every day,
   same food, same jokes, same friends, same everything.
"Oh, I wish something exciting would happen to me."
And one day
   she just decided
   she was gonna run away
   and make something exciting happen to her.
So she ran away,
   and she started walking,
   and she didn't tell anybody where she was going,
   and she walked all day long.
Oh, she was tired.

She thought,
    "You know, this is just as boring as staying at home.
    I think when I wake up, I'll go back home."
And she dozed,
    and she took a little nap,
    and when she woke up,
    she sat up,
    she looked down,
    and sitting at her feet,
    gals, I'm not kidding,
    there was the handsomest,
    best-looking young man.
Oh, my heavens.
Oh, her heart went like this—
    bump-a-bump-a-bump-a.
And she sat up,
    and gosh her hair wasn't—
    "Who are you?"
She thought,
    "Now, this is more like it. This is exciting stuff."
And he looked at her.
Oh, he was a hunk.
And he said,
    "I love you."
Oh, her heart really went fast.
He said,
    "I want to marry you.
    I want to take you to the valley of the butterflies,
    and take you to my home, and we will live happily ever after."
"Oh, I'm ready," she said.
She jumped up.
He said,
    "There's only one thing.
    When we go through the valley of the butterflies, you must not
        look at things."
    "Okay, no problem."
So here she goes,
    right behind him,

and he turned around, he said,
    "I'm not kidding."
He said,
    "They'll try to steal you from me. Do not look at the butterflies."
She said,
    "Okay. Fine. No problem."
So they started on,
    and they started to hear this music,
    like the best music that you could ever hear, and she said,
    "What is that?"
He said,
    "I told you, close your eyes, hold onto my belt.
    Don't look. Don't listen."
And he started walking faster.
Well, she closed her eyes and held onto his belt,
    and then they got louder and louder,
    and she thought,
    "Are those butterflies? Is that the music that I hear?"
And now she could smell,
    and it was the—
    any perfume that you've ever smelled, any shaving cologne—
    it was ten times better than that.
Better than the sweetest flower,
    the sweetest smell you've ever smelled.
It was better.
And she thought,
    "They couldn't hurt me if they smell like that
    and if they sound like that music.
    I'm just gonna peek a little bit."
And she opened her eyes,
    and the colors, oh, they were magnificent.
Oh, she just couldn't help it,
    she opened her eyes,
    and there were millions,
    not thousands, not hundreds, millions,
    and they were all around her.
She said,
    "They're so special, magnificent colors."

She just couldn't help it,
    she just let go of his belt,
    and she tried to catch just one or two,
    and they,
    they lightly kissed her like little tickles,
    like baby's kisses, it was so special.
She said,
    "Wait just a minute. Look at this, look at this."
He never looked back, he never said a word.
And she said,
    "Oh, I'll catch up with him in a minute."
And she took both hands off,
    and she was trying, and they were like laughing.
They weren't laughing,
    it was like little fairy laughing,
    they were just so special.
And she stopped,
    and she had them just all over her,
    and it was so neat.
She said,
    "I'll catch up with you in just a second.
    Oh, this is fantastic."
But he never stopped, he never looked back.
Now the millions of butterflies got on her,
    and they got heavier and heavier and heavier,
    and she said,
    "Now wait now."
And she tried to get them off,
    but they got heavier and heavier.
They got on her eyes,
    and closed her eyes, and she couldn't open her eyes.
She opened her mouth to call for help
    and ask him to come back and get them off her eyes,
    but when she opened her mouth, they went down her throat,
    and there were so many of them,
    and they filled her lungs,
    and she suffocated,
    and she died

in the valley of the butterflies.
And what this legend tells us,
  is:
  the next time you think your life is boring,
  and that you need to change and go for something really
      exciting,
  remember the grass is not always greener on the other side.
There's a lot of dangers out there
  that come disguised as beautiful and sweet smelling and nice
      sounding,
  but sometimes we're a lot better off at home.

›› Spearfinger

Okay.
We've got time for one more.
Have you ever watched a real scary movie?
Were you scared?
No.
What about when you went to bed and turned off the lights,
  did you look under the bed for monsters?
No.
How 'bout your closet?
Did you hear your dog outside and think Jason had come to kill
      you?
Well, you have to remember that those monsters are not real.
You can turn off the VCR any time.
You can walk out of the movie theater any time.
Turn on your light at any time, and the monsters are gone.
It's just in our imagination.
But a long long long time ago,
  those monsters were real.
And the worst one
  that the Cherokee people had
  was called
  Spearfinger.
She was awful.
She was forty feet tall,

and she was covered with this rock-like skin
  that no bullet, no weapon could penetrate.
And she was bloodthirsty.
She had one long,
  razor-sharp,
  spear finger,
  that she would slip up behind you,
  slip it through your back,
  pull out your liver,
  and eat it in one gulp.
She was covered with dried blood
  and snot, and gore dripped from her teeth.
She had razor-sharp teeth,
  she was vicious,
  and she was always coming around.
She loved to eat the flesh of young children
  more than anything.
And to get close to the children,
  she could change her shape.
She could turn and look just like your sister,
  just like your granny.
And as you were out picking blackberries
  or fishing or playing,
  your friend could disappear,
  and she would take his place,
  and you'd never know it until it was too late.
One day
  this village not far from here
  knew that Spearfinger was getting close to them.
And they just panicked.
  "What are we gonna do? Just let her walk in here and eat
      everybody?"
  "Well, I think we ought to fight her."
And they argued back and forth,
  "No, not me, I think we ought to run."
So they finally came up with a plan,
  that they would dig this huge pit
  all the way around the outside of the village

and cover it over with branches and trees and bushes,
    and when she fell into it,
    then they would try to kill her.
Everybody started helping.
They started digging,
    and everybody started helping,
    and moving rocks and getting the bushes.
And a young man,
    about your age,
    was really trying to help.
He was a little bit clumsy,
    'cause he was real excited.
He was trying to help,
    and he'd go to pull this, and he'd fall down.
He'd run get a big bucket of mud,
    and he'd spill it.
Finally,
    his dad got real aggravated with him
    and said,
    "Just go over there and sit.
    If you can't do any better than that, just get out of the way."
Oh, this really hurt his feelings,
    'cause he was just trying to help.
    "Golly, those little babies there, nobody's yelling at them, they
        fall down."
And went over,
    sat underneath the bushes,
    and he was just very upset.
He thought,
    "Spearfinger's coming,
    we all need to help,
    and nobody even wants to talk to me."
He felt real sorry for himself.
And he noticed
    that there was a little bird
    that was stuck in a honeysuckle vine
    and couldn't get loose.
But he was still real upset,

and not even thinking about the bird,
    he just gently let it loose,
    and was very surprised when the bird didn't fly off.
Instead,
    the bird came right on his shoulder
    and said,
    "I really thank you for helping me,
    and I'm gonna tell you a secret about Spearfinger.
    I know where her heart is."
      "She doesn't have a heart.
      You can't shoot her through the heart because it's all covered
          with rocks.
      Even our strongest warrior can't shoot through that."
    "No," she said,
    "The birds follow Spearfinger, and we know all of her secrets.
    We know where she hides,
    we know where her heart is
    'cause she doesn't fool with trying to eat us, we're too small.
    Look at the tip of her spear finger,
    and that's where her heart is.
    Shoot her there."
Oh, he was so excited,
    and he ran, and he said,
    "Dad, Dad, Dad, I know where her heart is."
The dad said,
    "I told you to get over there and sit down.
    I don't want to hear it."
And he ran over,
    and he tried to tell his mom,
    but before he could even tell anybody,
    they heard a horrible scream through the forest.
And it was Spearfinger.
And she was coming fast,
    and she was ravenously hungry.
Oh, she was screaming,
    and they ran and hid,
    and she fell into the pit,
    and they ran,

and they started trying to kill her,
  threw rocks at her,
  and she was just clawing her way up to the top.
Blood was just foaming at her mouth.
She was nasty.
And she was awful.
They knew that if she got loose she would kill everybody.
So they were trying to shoot her,
  shoot with bows and arrows,
  and they were screaming and running and trying to hide.
The little boy ran up to the strongest warrior and said,
  "Look at the tip of her spear finger."
And he looked,
  and it was just about as big as that,
  just tiny, just tiny.
He drew back
  and shot her right through the heart,
  and she fell over dead.
And after that the little boy was a great hero.
Everybody listened to him after that day.
Thank you.

›› The Birds and Animals Stickball Game

At one time,
  many years ago,
  human beings and animals
  could talk the same language
It was a very magic time.
And more than that,
  the animals and the birds
  could talk the same language, too.
They all had good times together,
  but occasionally they would argue.
Occasionally they would start to fight,
  and sometimes they would even hurt one another.
One day the birds argued with the animals
  that they were number one.

They were stronger, they were better, they were better looking.
They argued back and forth,
   and finally it almost broke into a war.
So they decided that they would do what the Cherokee men did:
   they would settle this by playing a game of stickball,
   and they set up the game.
Animals and birds came from miles around to bet on the game.
They were real excited.
This was going to be the battle to end all the arguments
   who was going to be number one forever.
And the game started.
First the birds scored,
   and then the animals scored,
   then the birds would score,
   then the animals would score,
   and finally it was tied up.
Eleven-eleven.
Whoever would score the next point would win the game,
   because the games end at twelve.
The birds got the ball, and they were streaking toward the goal,
   and they dropped it.
Oh, no.
The animals got the ball,
   and they threw it from one to another,
   and they finally threw it to their secret weapon,
   Mr. Skunk.
Mr. Skunk put that ball in his mouth,
   and he started waddling down the field,
   and everybody backed off.
Nobody wanted to tackle Mr. Skunk.
"Go for it, go for it, get the ball, he's gonna score."
Finally Mr. Buzzard, brave Mr. Buzzard, swooped down.
He grabbed the skunk so hard
   he ripped a white streak right down his back
      that he still has today.
And skunk sprayed him.
Oh, shoo, did he spray him.
He sprayed him so bad, and he stunk so much

that even today he flies all by himself,
all alone,
because he still stinks bad.
Oh, and Mr. Owl said,
    "No, I can do it, I can do it."
And he swooped down and he tried to get the ball and he got
            sprayed.
He got sprayed so bad it knocked rings around his eyes,
    and he still has those today.
Finally Mr. Bluejay said, "Watch me."
He swooped down all around the skunk's head,
    and the hummingbird swooped in real small
    and got the ball out of his mouth
    while the bluejay distracted him.
They went on and they scored the winning point.
The birds were so happy.
And Mr. Bluejay took all the credit—
    he knew he was the one
    that won that game.
So he went and he put a big sign hanging around all the trees
    that said the birds are number one.
And if you go out in the woods today,
    and you find a bluejay's nest,
    you look:
    and he'll have a piece of stringing hanging down
        right in the bottom of it
    as a signal to all the animals below
        that the birds are number one.

» The Cherokee Little People

There are a lot of stories and legends about the Little People.
You can see the people out in the forest.
They can talk, and they look a lot like Indian people
    except they're only about two feet high,
    sometimes they're smaller.
Now the Little People can be very helpful,
    and they can also play tricks on us, too.

And at one time there was a boy.
This boy never wanted to grow up.
In fact, he never wanted to grow up,
    and told everyone that so much
    that they called him "Forever Boy"
    because he never wanted to be grown.
When his friends would sit around and talk about:
    "Oh when I get to be a man, and when I get to be grown
    I'm gonna be this and I'm gonna go here and be this,"
    he'd just go off and play by himself.
He didn't even want to hear it,
    'cause he never wanted to grow up.
Finally his father got real tired of this,
    and he said,
    "Forever Boy, I will never call you that again.
    From now on you're going to learn to be a man,
    you're going to take responsibility for yourself,
    and you're going to stop playing all day long.
    You have to learn these things.
    Starting tomorrow, you're going to go to your uncle's,
    and he's going to teach you everything that you need to know."
Forever Boy was brokenhearted at what his father told him,
    but he could not stand the thought of growing up.
He went out to the river and he cried.
He cried so hard
    that he didn't see his animal friends gather around him.
And they were trying to tell him something,
    and they were trying to make him feel better,
    and finally he thought he understood them to say,
    "Come here tomorrow. Come here early."
Well, he thought they just wanted to say goodbye to him.
And he drug his feet going home.
He couldn't even sleep, he was so upset.
The next morning he went out early, as he had promised, to meet
        his friends.
And he was so sad,
    he couldn't even bear the thought of telling them goodbye
        forever.

Finally
    he began to get a sense that they were trying to tell him
            something else,
    and that is to look behind him.
And as he looked behind him,
    there they were—
    all the Little People—
    and they were smiling at him and laughing and running to hug
            him.
And they said,
    "Forever Boy, you don't have to grow up.
    You can stay with us forever.
    You can come and be one of us and you will never have to grow
            up."
"I can't do that. I have . . . my uncle's waiting on me.
    I can't do that. It would hurt my parents if I never came home
            again."
And they said,
    "No, we will ask the Creator to send a vision to your parents
    to let them know that you are safe and you are doing what you
            need to do."
Forever Boy thought about it for a long time.
But he decided that's what he needed to do.
And he went with the Little People.
And even today
    when you're out in the woods and you see something,
        and you look, and it's not really what you thought it was,
    or if you're fishing and you feel something on the end of your
            line,
    and you think it's the biggest trout ever,
    and you pull it in,
    and all it is is a stick that got tangled in your hook,
    that's what the Little People are doing.
They're playing tricks on you
    so you'll laugh and keep young in your heart.
Because that's the spirit of Little People, and Forever Boy,
    to keep us young in our hearts.

>> Nunnehí, the Gentle People

If you ever go out into the woods,
  and you think you hear someone talking,
  maybe some music,
  and you know there's no one else around you,
  there's a reason for that.
Out in the woods there live the gentle people.
And we call them the Cherokee word:
  Nunnehi.
The Nunnehi look a lot like Cherokee people,
  only they live underground
  in a special, special place.
One time, the Nunnehi came to the Cherokee people,
  and it was a very big surprise.
The Nunnehi men came to the head village and said,
  "You're going to have to come with us now.
  All of you pack up your belongings,
  and in seven days
  you will have to come with me
  and come and live with the Nunnehi."
Well, you can imagine what everyone was thinking.
"Why?"
"Where are we going to go?"
"Why do we have to go?"
"I don't want to go."
"Well, I want to go."
And they argued back and forth for days
  about what was going to happen.
They asked him on the seventh day
  where they were going and why.
He said,
  "Something terrible is going to happen.
  Worse than any flood
  or any famine
  that you have ever known before.
  Some dark and terrible day is coming,

and you have to leave now to save yourselves."
Well, when he said that,
   they decided to go with him.
So they packed up all their belongings,
   and they followed him for miles
   until they came to a big stone way deep in the mountains.
And as they watched, the stone rolled away.
They rushed to the entrance to see what was beyond there—
   to see where they were going.
And it was the most beautiful place that they had ever seen.
The most beautiful place that they could imagine.
The air just seemed to dance with joy.
It was beautiful.
Without even looking back,
   many families rushed ahead.
And as they turned to close the door forever,
   they saw a group standing way in the back.
The chief went over and asked them,
    "Why aren't you coming in?
   We're getting ready to close the door.
   You have to come now."
But the old people in the group said,
"We were born here,
   and no matter what happens we want to stay."
The young people said,
    "We want our children to be born
   here in the mountains
   where our grandparents were born.
   And we've decided to stay."
He was torn between going with this group and staying.
He decided that he needed to stay,
   that whatever bad was coming,
   he needed to stay and help lead his people.
The stone rolled over,
   and we've never seen or heard from them again.
The others remained,
   and these are the ones that we're descended from.
The bad part

was the Trail of Tears removal
that forced thousands of people to leave this area and go to
        Oklahoma.
So if the Nunnehi ever come again,
    we know something bad is going to happen
    and will have to decide what to do then.
Remember that as you're out in the woods
    you might hear something,
    you might hear some music,
    you might hear someone talking,
    and it's the Nunnehi,
    and they're reminding us
    that they're always with us.

➤ Davey Arch

Davey Arch was born in Cherokee in 1957. He now lives in nearby Waynesville with his wife and son but spends every day with his mother and his grandfather in Cherokee. He makes his living by selling his carvings, which often are masks, made of different kinds of wood, that represent the seven clans. Occasionally he carves a mask representing someone he knows or some aspect of one of the stories he tells. Davey also speaks about Cherokee culture to school-teachers and other groups, and he tells stories—folktales, legends, and narratives about his grandfather's life.

Davey learned to tell stories from his immediate and extended family. In addition to the traditional Cherokee tales and stories about history, Davey's grandfather, who read widely, liked to tell Uncle Remus stories. Davey tells stories in a relaxed, soft-spoken style, sometimes working on his carvings while he is speaking.

"In the past," he says, "the Cherokees used storytelling and legends and communicating in that way to educate and even to pass on our history. There were several ways that the Cherokees told stories. A lot of times in the evening, after the evening meal, everyone would gather around the elders, and the elders would maybe take down their pipe and smoke a little bit or maybe have some tobacco that they would chew, and kind of relax and sit around. And then they would start telling the stories.

"Sometimes if there were a lot of children around, the stories would emphasize the lessons they needed to learn so that they would be able to live as good human beings in this life. Other times the stories were only told to the certain people who were in line for this information: people who practiced medicine, and the history keepers. Those who were to keep the history alive would go and study almost as an apprentice with the history keepers and the storytellers.

"And in this way our history was kept by word of mouth and passed from generation to generation. And today this is something that is very important still to us because the same stories that have been passed down for thousands of years still teach the same vital lessons that people need to be good human beings and to understand what it takes to live in the world that surrounds them.

"A lot of times the stories were only told in certain settings. For instance, the priests and shamans only told stories to the people that were in line to receive this knowledge. Sometimes these stories were only told in the council houses or the sacred places.

"And then there were other stories, general stories that were used to teach lessons but in a lighthearted way. A lot of times this is the best way. People are more susceptible to something if it makes them laugh than if it scares them or teaches a lesson in a negative way.

"So there's a lot of ways we've used this, but it was the most important factor in keeping our history alive. The legend telling and the oral history was probably the most important thing in keeping our traditions and our culture alive and our identity as being Cherokee, being the people that we are.

"And today this is still very important to me, knowing where we came from and who we came from and how they believed and how they thought and how they considered life. All these things were conveyed through the legends and the stories.

"And today to sit and listen to the old folks talk about the things of the past—and even things in recent times that have sprung stories and helped us to understand and how to deal with everyday situations—is a continuation of a tradition that started thousands of years ago with our people with oral history keeping and legend telling."

Davey recognizes that changes in the way people live have affected storytelling traditions. "Today everyone has their own house, and they have their own room in their own house, and they have their own television in their own room in their own house. So no one eats a meal together, no one does the same recreation together. In my house up here in Cherokee, I don't even have a television in the house. I just refuse to have it. In Waynesville, at our house over there, there's a television in every room. It's just a constant noise and different distraction from room to room. And you know, I enjoy technology and things like computers and television, but a lot of people, you know, never understand that they really have to get away from that a little while and be exposed to something else to really get the full flavor of life."

Because the extended family and storytelling evenings aren't as common as they were in the recent past, Davey comments, "Well, the extended family being displaced has dramatically cut into the tradition of storytelling, and the oral tradition of history keeping, and passing along your lineage through sitting around talking about your relatives."

Instead, storytelling seems more sharply divided between those who tell stories at home among their families and those who choose to concentrate on telling stories in public, outside the Cherokee community. "What's happened in this community is that storytellers are becoming people who research stories, and go and interview people and seek out these stories so that they can keep this tradition alive. And in a lot of communities these people sometimes feel that they need to do this, as doing their part in preserving the culture. Some people are making a living at it. And some people get into it, like myself."

Davey has seen the revival of pride in traditional ideas through the schools' Cherokee language and traditional arts programs. "When you get children coming home asking questions about things that they've been exposed to at school, it's just automatic for the parent to tell them what they know and to relate stories and feelings. And so I'm sure, you know, that it will continue to exist but not really be practiced as it has in the past."

>>

Davey's stories were collected on a rainy April morning in the exhibit room of the Qualla Arts and Crafts Co-op and during a June videotaping session on the Blue Ridge Parkway. These stories include two of the tales most often told by Cherokee storytellers, "The

Origin of Strawberries" and "How the Possum Lost His Tail," both found in James Mooney's collection, but the others are unique. Some were told to him by his grandfather, who was born in 1909 and raised in a very traditional manner in Cherokee, and others are Davey's own stories about his grandfather's life.

Stories from Davey's grandfather include "The Old Man and the Birds" (about the origin of the blowgun), "The Brave, the Mighty Warrior," and "The Strange Husband." Of these, only "The Strange Husband" (or "The Owl Man") is in Mooney's collection. The rest of Davey's tales describe events in his grandfather's life, beginning with a story about Cherokee medicine, "Grandpa and the Turtle." "The Rattlesnake in the Corn" also describes the activities of a medicine man, Ute, and his relationship with the natural world. Davey's other stories—about the Removal, about war for the Cherokees, about the Uk'tena, about the old cities of refuge—are all part of Cherokee oral history; they are the stories that have kept alive information about the past of the Cherokee people.

When Davey talks about growing up in Cherokee and about things that happened to his grandfather and grandmother as children, we can see some of the experiences of Cherokee people over nearly a hundred years. When Davey's grandfather was a young man, he logged and made a living from the woods, as did many others. He made moonshine, as others did. Davey's grandmother, however, was a strict Baptist. "My grandfather always had me on the mountain or down at the creek into some kind of meanness, and my grandmother was always teaching me the right way, or the way to be accepted in any culture." Some Scots-Irish families in the mountains were like this, too, with "Baptists and bootleggers" joined in marriage or by blood, but the Cherokees' values and traditions made their life experiences as different from those of their white neighbors as biscuits are from bean bread.

Events of the early twentieth century cast their shadows on these tales—the flu epidemic of 1918, other serious diseases, and a logging accident orphaned both Davey's grandfather and grandmother, who were raised by their respective aunts and uncles. Davey's account of growing up in Cherokee in the mid-twentieth century, surrounded by cousins, also gives us insight into the town of Cherokee and the effects of tourism during the last century, as well as other changes in lifestyle that have affected all Americans. Within these accounts are embedded other stories from family tradition, such as "Jeannie and the Booger" and Grandpa's exploding jars— stories like those told in other families but unique to this time and place and culture. And as always with Cherokee stories, humor plays an important role in keeping us all in balance.

▸▸ **Grandpa and the Turtle**

This morning I was thinking of some stories I'd been told growing up, by my grandfather, real-life events, true stories, things that have happened to him early in the twentieth century.

▸▸

He was raised by his aunt and his uncle,
    which was pretty traditional around here at the turn of the
        century.
There were several diseases that were causing a lot of kids to
        become orphans.
Polio was bad, and the flu epidemics were real bad.
So a lot of children were displaced because of that.
And my grandfather's brothers and sisters had become sick
    and a couple of them had died, when they were real young.
And his mother and his father had passed away, too.
His father was killed in a logging accident.
And so his aunt and uncle, Juliss and Stacey, raised him.
And when his brothers and sisters started becoming sick,
    his uncle contacted a medicine man named Mink.
And grandpa said old man Mink would come and stay with them,
    you know,
    when he was passing through that part of the country.
I'm not sure where he lived.
I don't know whether he was from Robbinsville or somewhere else
        around.
But Grandpa said that in anticipation of Mink coming for a visit,
    his Uncle Juliss caught a mud turtle and kept it.
And they used a mud turtle for medicine,
    to make people live longer.

And so when Mink came, the next visit, he had the mud turtle
      ready.
And my grandpa said that Mink took him to the—
    Soco Creek ran out in front of their house—
    he took him out to the creek and sang.
And he spoke only in Cherokee,
    and said he sang what we call formulas or prayers.
And said Mink had some beads,
    he said he had red and black and white beads
      made out of stone,
    he said he had them wrapped up in a red handkerchief.
And said during this ceremony that they were going through,
    he said he laid this handkerchief out beside the water
      right at a little eddy at the edge of the creek
      where the water was kind of still.
And he said he spoke something to the beads,
    and they rolled off of that handkerchief
    and got out on top of the water
    and just started kind of dancing around.
And he said this went on for a while.
He said that he took the mud turtle
    and cut its head off
    and made Grandpa drink a spoonful
      of that turtle blood
      during all this.
And said they stayed out there a long time.
And he said finally his Aunt Stacey called them for supper,
    or for a meal.
And he said that Mink said something,
    and those beads came off the water
    and came back up onto that red handkerchief.
And he said they gathered up their stuff
    and went on back to the house.
And he said that, you know, he's been sick
    and had all kinds of things happen to him
    but he's outlived a lot of his family.
You know, he's outlived a son, and his wife, and several
      grandchildren,

and all of his brothers and sisters and aunts and uncles
and people like that.
And he was raised to believe in that kind of medicine
and was raised very traditionally.
He's got a lot of stories like that, you know.
And he looks at it as being fairly insignificant when he looks back
on it, you know,
but it really impacted his life.
And he's eighty-five now.
And he's had quite a few major operations.
He's had a kidney taken out
and has plastic veins in his legs.
He's had his liver operated on
and had part of his stomach taken out once.
And you know,
it's just all kinds of things that have happened to him,
and he's all scarred up.
And he says he's like an old turtle:
when you find an old turtle
you'll find his shell all skinned up and scarred up.
But he said that's the way he is,
he's going to live a long time,
but he'll be all scarred up. [laughs]

▸ **The Rattlesnake in the Corn**

That corn over there reminds me of a story he told me
about a man that he used to stay with named Ute Jumper.
Ute was kind of a medicine man or a conjure man too,
and Grandpa said that he would stay with him
a lot of times during, I guess, his teenaged years.
And he said that Ute was all the time amazing him with something,
you know.
He said one time the corn had got up and was beginning to get
ripe,
and Ute told him
to come with him,
and he'd show him something.

Said Ute took him up on the mountain
    where his cornfields were at.
Said up above his cornfields
    there was a big rock bar in the mountains,
    real rocky, and a lot of rocks.
Said when he left
    he'd gotten some milk and some cornbread
    to take with them.
And he said when he got up to this rock bar,
    he called a snake out of the rocks.
Said it was a big yellow rattlesnake,
    said he sang to it
    and fed it this cornbread and milk.
And after he'd fed the snake,
    then he sang to it again
    and asked it in Cherokee
    if it would watch his corn for him.
And said the snake went out into the cornfield
    in front of him.
He said when they got out in the middle of the cornfield,
    he sang to it again.
And Grandpa said the snake stayed in that cornfield
    all that fall,
    till they cut the corn
    and got it all in.
And he said that was to keep the rats
    and the ground squirrels
    and the squirrels
    out of the corn.
Said it kept him out of the corn, too!
Said when he was sent after roasting ears
    he'd pick from around the edge. [laughs]

›› Big Snakes

Grandpa tells a lot of stories about big rattlesnakes
    that were in these mountains
    and big water snakes.

He said it wasn't uncommon at all
    to see an eight- or ten-foot-long snake, you know,
    these big water snakes, big black snakes.
He said the largest rattlesnake he ever saw
    he said was up in Hornbuckle Valley.
He said he'd fished up Hornbuckle Creek,
    which is just right above our house.
He had a little dog,
    and he said coming back out of the woods
        from fishing that day,
    he was walking down this logging road,
    and he said it was right before dark.
He said they walked around a curve
    and in a little straight
    in the road in front of them—
    he said it looked like a tree limb had fallen
    and was laying, he said,
    from up on the bank in the woods
    all the way across the road
And he said a log truck had unloaded a whole lot of logs there
    right below the road.
Evidently they'd had a flat tire
    or a chain had broke or something.
But he said this big log pile was right below the road.
And he said he would have walked right up on this snake,
    said it was a big snake laying there,
    but his dog started barking at it.
And he said once the dog started barking,
    he said he stopped,
    and he could smell the snake.
Rattlesnakes, and copperheads too,
    give off a real kind of distinct odor.
And he said, once he realized what it was,
    he said he was afraid to try to go past it,
    said he was afraid to try to kill it
    because it was so large.
He said he felt kind of trapped there, you know,
    said it was getting dark,

and he didn't want to go up and around
  on the mountain.
So he said finally he took a big rock,
  he said, about big as he could lift.
He thought, I'll just break its back
  and maybe that'll kill it and it'll—
  or get it to go over the bank or something.
He said he threw the rock at it
  and missed the snake.
He said the rock hit across in the road.
But he said
  the snake felt the rock hit the ground
  and said it moved
  and went on off into that big log pile.
Said he went on around it,
  went on down the road.
He said it must have been twelve or fifteen feet long,
  and it was about as big around as his leg.
I've never seen any big snakes like that,
  but I've seen a snake skin
  that used to be in an old grocery store up here on Soco
  and it was about eight or ten feet long,
  and it was tacked on a board,
  and in the middle of the skin,
  I guess it was a foot or maybe fifteen inches wide,
  you know the skin was, where it flattened out.
There used to be a fellow named Cub that worked with Grandpa.
They used to cut a lot of acid wood for the tanneries,
  and they cut the chestnut timber,
  and they also hewed railroad ties.
Grandpa logged with ox, all the time,
  so they'd take these yoke of oxen,
  go up in the woods and pull out laurel and rhododendron
      stumps.
And these were sold to pipe manufacturing companies,
  they make tobacco pipes out of these burls,
  and that was something that he and Cub did.
But Cub lived across the mountain, on Jenkins Creek,

and we live on Soco Creek,
   right at the mouth of Hornbuckle Creek.
There's a gap in the mountain,
   right straight above the house,
    called Jumper Gap.
And Cub would walk up from his house
   and walk into Jumper Gap in the mornings
   and rest before he came on down to Grandpa's house,
   before they went to work.
He said one morning Cub come in the house,
   said he just come bolting through the door
   out of breath
   and just pale.
Said he thought he'd been snakebit or something himself.
But he said once he finally got him calmed down to see what
        happened—
   he'd got into the gap that morning
   and set down
   on a snake.
Thought it was a pole, laying across the trail.
And just walked up, he said, just stepped across it and set back on it
   and it started moving. [chuckles]
So, I don't know whether it was the same snake that Grandpa had
        seen
   or whether there was that many large snakes
    in the mountains
   that now, because of development and, you know,
   people not having *any* tolerance for snakes,
   there's not hardly any anymore.
It's very rare to see a rattlesnake or a copperhead
   or even a big black snake anymore.

Grandpa said a snake bit his cow one time,
   and it was only about six feet long
   and knocked his cow down
   when it bit it.
Said it got the cow down on the ground.
Bit it on the hind leg, he said,

about four feet off the ground.
Snake jumped and hit the cow that high.
And he said the cow went plumb down on the ground,
   so I'm sure it'd knock a man down, you know.
There have been several people around here bitten by snakes.
My great-aunt, my Aunt Annie, my grandmother's sister,
   was bitten on the calf of the leg
   with a copperhead once.
And I remember I was pretty young, maybe six or eight years old.
And they'd keep alcohol packs on her leg
   seemed like all summer that summer.
And her leg turned black.
I can remember that just like it was yesterday,
   how they done wrapped that leg
   and the whole calf of her leg was just black,
   just black as coal,
   looked like a big bruise or something.
But she got better and lived another twenty-five years, I guess,
   after that happened, another twenty years, I guess.
So there's a lot of people around that have had experiences like that.
I guess that's why there's not much tolerance for snakes.
But you know, a long time ago,
   the Cherokees considered the rattlesnake their brother
   and revered it
   as probably the most dangerous thing in Cherokee country.
So they wouldn't kill a rattlesnake when they found it.
And just like Ute having that one that he kept to guard his corn,
   they had an association
   and a realization of how the snake was
   and how it wanted to be dealt with, I guess.
And I think that kind of understanding was pretty widespread
   among all plants and animals.
The Cherokees had an understanding.
That's why they could use so many plants for medicine
   and why so many things had a specific use
   instead of just—
   today when people build or garden or do a lot of things
   it's just kind of in a haphazard way.

They've got the general information
    but not really the specific information
    that used to govern how things were done
    and what time.
And a lot of that information
    that used to be everyday common knowledge
    has really died out quickly in this community.

▸▸ The Old Man and the Birds

This is a mask with a bird flying out of the man's mouth,
    and this is a story that my grandfather told me
    a long time ago
    when I was just a young boy.
He said that
    way way back before the invention of the blowgun,
    there was an old man who had become old and feeble,
    and he was too old to hunt,
    too old to go to the river and fish,
    he was afraid he would fall on the rocks and hurt himself.
All that he was really able to do
    was to go out and tend his garden each day.
And this was the only food that he was able to get for himself.
He knew that the vegetables
    and the things that he grew in his garden were good for him,
    and they would sustain life,
    but he craved the taste of meat in with his vegetables.
So he prayed
    and asked the Supreme Being if he would help him
    in his quest to have something beside the food he could raise in
        his garden.
So in his dreams that night
    the Supreme Being sent the Little People.
They entered into the dream world of this old man.
In his dream world they showed him how to make a blowgun,
    how to fashion the darts.
And they instructed him
    that if he would go out into his cornfields and sit and wait,

the birds that were coming to steal his corn
would be the victims of the new blowgun that he had made.
So the next morning
   when the old man awoke,
   he fashioned a blowgun,
   tied the darts.
It took him a time or two of practice
   before he could get a dart that would fly true.
But he was proud of the invention
   the Little People had taught him to make.
He thought he would try it out.
So he hobbled out into his cornfield,
   sat down still,
   and waited for the birds to come.
Just regular as clockwork,
   here came the birds.
When they got into the corn
   he was able to shoot them with his new blowgun.
He would take the birds back to his house,
   he would clean the birds,
   wash them good,
   and roast them in front of the fireplace.
He would roast them
   until they were so hard no one could bite them.
They were just like a piece of jerky or dried meat.
He would store these birds and keep them till he needed them.
The way he prepared these birds,
   he would take these birds out
   and pound them up in his pounding block that he made
         cornmeal in,
   pound them up into a fine powder.
In the mornings
   when he would make his porridge out of the corn,
   he would season it with some of the birds he had killed out of
         his cornfield.
This was some of the finest food that he had ever tasted.
He began to really enjoy this.
And soon he was eating this every day.

He would season his food
   with the birds that he killed out of his cornfield.
But each day
   he would kill more birds than he needed,
   so he stored these birds in the corner next to the fireplace
   where they would stay dry.
This went on for a long time,
   and he was enjoying his food
   and felt the Supreme Being had showed him the way
   he would have meat with his vegetables.
So this went on,
   and one day
   a man passing smelled the birds and the corn soup cooking.
And he went over and asked the old man
   if he might have some of this fine-smelling food
   that he had smelled while passing by his farm.
The old man agreed that he would give him some,
   and he sat him down at the table and fed him.
But the man who came by was a thief,
   and he looked around
   and saw that the old man had all these birds stored in a corner
   next to the fireplace, had big baskets of corn sitting in the corner.
So the thief thought,
   "This old man is not going to live much longer,
   he doesn't need all this food,"
   so he killed the old man.
And after he had killed the old man,
   he ate up what the old man had fixed of the soup
   and began to try to prepare his own soup.
But each time that he would try to fix the birds,
   he would put the whole bird into the soup.
And every time he would get a bird out to eat,
   to put into his mouth,
   the bird would change back into a live bird
   and fly out of his mouth.
And this was the way that the Little People had of tricking the thief.
And in the end,
   the thief wasn't able to eat any of the food

that he had stolen from the old man.
And in the end,
    he too starved to death and died
    from killing the old man and stealing his food.

Grandpa was trying to emphasize to me
    that you shouldn't do evil for selfish gains,
    like the thief that had stolen the old man's food,
    thinking that he would be able to eat the food and survive.
The Little People had put a spell on the food that the old man
        gathered,
    and each time the thief would try to eat,
    the birds would turn back into live birds and fly away.
So he starved to death.
Grandpa was telling me
    that bad deeds will return to you,
    that the evil you do will come back against you.
The thief should have been thankful for the food that the old man
        had given him
    and left him in peace instead of doing him the way that he done.

›› The Brave, the Mighty Warrior

When I was a young boy, this is what my grandfather told me.
He said,
    once there was a brave warrior,
    one of the mightiest warriors that ever lived,
    who began to become very arrogant, proud of what he'd done,
    and began to boast
    to all the people in his village
    of how mighty a warrior he was.
And even though they knew of his reputation
    and knew of the deeds that he had done in battle,
    he still persisted on telling them how great he was
    and boasting how much better he was at being a warrior than
        the other warriors.
And soon
    this was something that became very annoying

to a lot of the people around the village
and to the other warriors.
But still the brave warrior,
   the mighty warrior,
   persisted in boasting.
He began to think about the weapons and tools that he used in his
          work,
   and he began to fashion the best tools of anyone in the village.
His war club was the best of any war club that had ever been made,
   his bow was the strongest bow,
   and his arrows began to be the best arrows
      that anyone had ever seen.
He'd chip his arrow points to just a razor-sharp edge,
   fasten them onto the shafts,
   so that they would fly just as true as any arrow ever flew.
But still he boasted
   and went on and on
   with how great he was
   and how great the things that he used was.
The old men began to warn him
   that his boasting would cause him failure in the end.
But he didn't heed the warnings and went on boasting.
Soon the tribe went to war with another enemy,
   and the brave warrior
   gathered up his fine tools of the trade
   and went off to war.
But in the battle
   he was knocked unconscious from behind
   by one of his enemies
   and taken captive.
And all the things that he had carried with him into battle
   were taken with him into the enemies' camp.
When the enemy saw
   what he had been using against them,
   they decided that these would be the things
   that would be used in his demise.
So they tied the mighty warrior up
   and shot him with his own arrows.

My grandfather told me this story
   hoping that I would understand
   that in planning life and arranging things
   that a man,
   even though he might accomplish things,
   should not boast of what he's done.
And in planning to do things
   and in planning your life
   and the strategies
     of how you will accomplish your life's journey,
   you should be wary
   that in the end
   you won't be shot with your own arrows.

» The Strange Husband (The Owl Man)

Traditionally
   our masks weren't used to really tell stories
   in the way that I've been using the masks
   that I've made recently to tell stories.
Traditionally
   our masks were used in our dances and for our medicine.
But in the same light,
   a lot of our stories taught a lesson
   and were used in our medicine also.
And a lot of times
   when I'm sitting around carving,
   I'll begin to think of the stories that I've been told.
One story that came to mind
   one day when I was carving
   was the story of the man
   who wasn't bringing anything home in the evenings for supper
   but things like mice and frogs
   and maybe a snake or a lizard or a crawfish
   or something along those lines.
His wife couldn't understand this,
   and she began to question him,

"Why don't you bring home food like bear and deer and other
      game,
or fish like all the other hunters?"
But he never would tell her.
So one day
    she decided she would follow him
    when he went hunting
    and find out what he was up to.
And as she followed him down to the river this morning,
    he stopped at the water and began a ceremony,
    and through this ceremony
    he transformed himself into an owl.
And each day
    he had been turning into an owl
    and hunting as an owl
    during the daytime.
And in the evening
    when he would return home
    he would change himself back into a man.
But all he would have to show
    for his day's effort of hunting
    would be the owl food.
So this is a mask I've carved
    with a frog in its mouth
    to kind of emphasize
    the story of the man who was bringing home owl food for supper.

›› Legends of the Uk'tena

There's quite a few stories around about the Uk'tena.
And not long ago, maybe ten years ago,
    there was a crystal found, over on Tellico Plains,
    when they were doing the excavation over there,
    that was a crystal like the Uk'tena was supposed to have guarded.
And they found this crystal wrapped in a full deerskin
    and put away the way it was supposed to have been
    when it was put away not to be used anymore.

And when they were using this crystal
    they had to feed it.
Then they had a formula or a prayer to put it to sleep with
    when it wasn't going to be used.
But Uk'tena was the giant snake that was supposed to have guarded
        this.
And there's a lot of stories about Uk'tena through the mountains
    how large and fierce it was
And there's stories of it being a giant rattlesnake,
    that I've heard.
And there's other stories about it being a horned serpent,
    a serpent with horns.
So I don't know whether there were two types of snakes that large
    in this part of the country
    or what it was.
And there's also stories about the people who lived in the
        underworld
    that rode giant rattlesnakes.
And the entrance to this underworld
    was through the rivers and the streams.
They would go into the big pools in the rivers,
    go into the passages that led into the underworld
    where the snakes were large enough to ride like horses.

➤➤ Removal

Solomon Bird is a man I know in Robbinsville.
And I went to visit him a few summers ago,
    took my grandfather down there
    and Mike Kline, who was working as a folklorist up at
    Western, was with us.
And it was really funny.
Mike had gone to visit Solomon on an occasion before we went.
And Solomon had used his granddaughter as an interpreter,
    and wouldn't speak English to Mike.
So Mike thought that Solomon couldn't speak English.
So it was funny, when we got to his house that day,
    he came out

and he knew that I didn't speak enough Cherokee
to communicate in Cherokee.
And Grandpa is more comfortable with English now than he is
Cherokee,
even though he does speak it fairly fluently.
Realizing this, Solomon, when he came out,
just started talking in English,
and [laughs] Mike's mouth fell open.
He was really floored by it.
But Solomon told us a story that day,
of his grandmother,
who had lived on the road where he lived,
on up the road there.
And when the soldiers came through and rounded up the people,
they had taken his grandmother and her parents
at gunpoint
and marched them down the road,
right in front of Solomon's house.
And you know, to hear him talk about that,
and relate the story that his grandmother told him
about that specific place right there in front of his house.
It was really a touching thing and caused me to realize how—
how close, that this had happened not so long ago.
It was recent history
and not prehistoric,
things that we kind of generalize about,
that this was a true story.
His grandmother had stayed captive for three days
before they had escaped and come back up into that part of the
country
there in Little Snowbird.
And there was a lot of people like that, I think,
who were rounded up.
And this valley, that goes up the Valianniner River here, was very
populated,
there was a huge town through here.
And they came in and rounded everybody up at gunpoint and
marched them out.

And this was something that I don't think a lot of Cherokees were
           aware of.
I think a lot of people didn't have a whole lot of communication
    with what was going on at the time
    and so they were totally taken by surprise, a lot of them, I think.
And children—
    like Solomon's grandmother—
    had no idea what was going on.
It was just a very traumatic scary time.
They thought they were all going to be killed
    because they all knew the stories
    of the British coming through and exterminating the villages.
So these,
    when the army came in with guns to march them out,
    I'm sure these stories about the atrocities that had happened in
        the past
    just kind of flashed to their minds.
And the worst things imaginable
    probably were really preying on these people's minds.
And some really catastrophic things did happen
    to a lot of people that were rounded up.
Now Solomon, when he told the story, really conveyed a lot of
    emotion.
This was something that he felt was a crime that had been committed
    against him as well as his grandmother
    because of how she told him the story.
So there still are a lot of people who still remember the Removal
    that clearly.

➤➤ War

The village up there where Judaculla Rock is,
    all that village was destroyed,
    five hundred homes in that village.
They killed everybody
    and burnt their village to the ground.
Probably killed twenty-five hundred, three thousand people that day.
All the houses they excavated had dead people in them.

You know, they just come in and shot them, mostly.
Left them in the house and burned the houses down.
During that time that they were being moved out
    was when they were supposed to have moved some sacred
        objects
      out of that city up there too.
There was a frog, a carved stone frog,
    that was supposed to have been something with a lot of power,
    I don't know what kind of power,
    but it was supposed to have been moved
    and had a curse put on it
    that whoever dug it back up would have a bad time after that.
And there was another big village down here at Ela,
    was about that same size.
They estimate maybe five thousand people lived in that village,
    huge village.
And then the towns down in north Georgia and around
    were also some pretty big villages.
I've never heard many stories about towns north of here.

Grandpa told me a story once that Mink had told him.
This was in pre-Columbian times.
That a tribe from up north,
    somewhere in Virginia or West Virginia, maybe,
    had come down into northern Cherokee country
    and raided some villages and taken some slaves
    and had killed some women and children.
So they said out of vengeance
    the Cherokee nation went together
    and went up and completely exterminated that tribe,
    killed every one in the whole tribe.
So it wasn't only non-Indians committing these atrocities
    against the Indians.
This kind of behavior was universal.
No matter whether you were Indian or non-Indian
    or African or Asian or whatever.
You know, this kind of thing, human beings been human beings
    since the beginning of time.

➤➤ **Women**

The whole idea of the role that women played
    in different cultures and societies in Native American tribes
    was very different from tribe to tribe.
Like out west in some of those tribes, the nomadic tribes,
    the women weren't much more than just a work force.
You know.
And the struggle for survival was so intense,
    and war was such a part of everyday life
    that the women played a completely different role in that culture
    than they did in this culture.
Here, women decided whether we would go to war or not,
    which was totally opposite from some of the Plains tribes.
And some of our neighboring tribes, too,
    that practiced a lot of slavery and piracy and things like that
    had a different regard toward women.
But most of the southeastern cultures really had a reverence for
        women
    because they were the continuation of life
    and were sacred in that aspect.
And that's basically how, I think, the Cherokees believed.
And that's why, through eons,
    the women, you know,
    really became an integral part of medicine and religion and the
        whole culture.
And everything was interconnected, too,
    so that separating anything,
    one way or another,
    was for a specific reason.
There was things like,
    if you're a ball player,
    you're not supposed to let women ever touch the sticks
        that you're going to play ball with.
So there was extremes in regard to women, like that.
One way or another,
    for a specific reason.

» Cities of Refuge

And we had cities of refuge,
    where people would go in times of war.
And it was strange,
    they would keep a woman on her menstrual cycle
    at the gates of these cities to guard the gates.
And I don't know whether it was something respected by a lot of
        tribes,
    that you didn't go past or violate a woman during this time or—.
And at that same time,
    women aren't supposed to be in the garden.
So that was traditional, among the Cherokees.
So it could have been that that northern tribe
    just had no regard for women and children in that aspect.
Or it might have been just a group of those from that tribe,
    just a radical gang
    that had come in to try to prove something
    and things got out of hand.
And it could have been that kind of circumstance,
    but anyway, that tribe no longer exists
    because of the vengeance of the Cherokee.

Nikwasi was one of the cities of refuge.
Most of these cities were stockaded cities.
They had communal storehouses in these cities where the excess,
    kind of like a tax,
    was taken by the civil chiefs and stored in these storehouses.
And it was also kind of like a social security system.
Handicapped people, cripples, and orphans,
    and elderly without family to take care of them
    were provided for by the civil chief
    in these storehouse kind of operations.
And in times of crop failure, drought, or in times of war,
    things like this,
    they also had a food supply that they didn't have to worry about.
And I think because of tribes storing goods like that,

piracy and slavery was really common amongst southeastern
Indians.
I know there's a lot of stories about the Creek,
to the south of us,
coming up to raid Cherokee villages for stored goods and for
slaves.
And we have stories of slaves in our tribe
that were sometimes adopted into the tribe and treated as equals.
Sometimes they were set free to go back to where they were from.
And at other times, after the job was done, they were put to death.
And this was also something, that was an issue,
that the women decided on.
The Beloved Woman and her council of women really had a lot of
control.
And it's just basic logic the way that I look at it.
Some things are just easier done that way.
Women's sense of ethics and morality toward life
and things like that
were very much different than men.

›› The Origin of Strawberries

One of my favorite stories,
that Mary Chiltoskey used to tell,
is the story of the origin of the strawberries.
And she said that first man and woman were living together,
and they got mad at one another, and the man left.
No, the woman left, that's the way it was.
And went to live somewhere else.
The man began to miss her, so he prayed.
And God told him about the strawberries,
and told him he would line the trail along to where the woman
was staying,
and she would begin to eat the strawberries,
follow the trail of strawberries back to where he was at.
And they were reunited.
They say that's why the strawberries bloom so early in the spring,
they're the first berry,

they come out,
they were the first berry that man presented to woman,
to gain her affection, or regain her affection.
And all the old people
keep some strawberry preserves around
to remind them
and to keep peace in the house.

>> **How the Possum Lost His Tail**

And you know the stories that taught lessons were usually just short
stories
about something that happened to an animal
because he was rude, or arrogant or something.
One my favorites—
when possum lost the hair off of his tail,
because of being so arrogant
that he was bragging and being a nuisance to the rest of the
animals.
So they decided to trick the possum,
and decided to have a dance in his honor.
And the rabbit went to him
and told him what they had planned
and the possum thought that was a good idea,
that he'd be able to really brag and show off his beautiful tail.
At that time
he had the most beautiful tail in all the animal kingdom.
And so the rabbit told him
that in preparation for the dance
he needed to fix himself up,
and called the crickets to prepare his tail for the dance that night.
And he told the rabbit
that as the crickets worked,
that they would wrap his tail in bark,
so that it wouldn't be messed up before he got to the dance.
And in reality
what the crickets were doing
were cutting the hair off of his tail

and hiding the bare tail with bark as they cut the hair off.
And so
    they got his tail all wrapped up and got him ready for the dance.
That night at the dance when possum came in,
    everyone stopped and was looking at the possum.
And he came to the middle of the dance floor,
    and untied his tail,
    and when the naked tail hit the floor,
    all the animals started to laugh.
And he looked back and saw what had happened,
    and out of embarrassment
    he fell over,
    pretended he was dead.
Even today
    he doesn't have any hair on his tail,
    and still plays dead when he's embarrassed or frightened.
You know,
    stories like that are humorous stories
    that kids will pay attention to and listen to.
And then after the story
    you can tell them that this is the kind of thing
    that will happen to you
    if you brag and are pretentious around your peers.

›› Growing Up in Cherokee

The extended family
    when I was growing up
    was a big part of everybody's life.
I can remember there being just a yardful of my cousins
    at my grandparents' house.
And we lived with my grandparents
    until I was about ten years old
    in a four-room house.
There were like always eight or ten people there.
And so everybody slept together.
And there were two bedrooms and a kitchen and a living room.
And everybody set around.

I remember we had a television,
    but everybody had something to do while they were sitting there.
You were either peeling fruit or stringing beans or making
        something.
And you had daily chores that had to be done.
And everybody had their part to play.
I was talking to my son the other day.
He was helping me take out the garbage.
And I told him that when I was growing up
    we didn't have garbage,
    we fed scraps to the chickens or the hogs,
    we burned the paper,
    most of our food was canned in Mason jars,
    and we used those over again.
The food you ate didn't come in a prepackaged deal,
    it was something that you bought in bulk and stored,
    or something that you got out of the can house,
    or out of the basement,
    or out of the root cellar, and prepared.
And I can remember the first time I ate a pizza,
    I was about, probably, eight years old,
    and this guy name Joe Sweet
    had opened a little hamburger stand and pizza parlor down here
        in Cherokee.
And my grandmother and I would walk
    from church here in town back over to her house,
    and after church a lot of times
    we'd stop by one of the restaurants and have lunch.
And one day we stopped and had a pizza for lunch.
But that was a novelty,
    really something to me.
You grew your own livestock and chickens.
We kept a lot of animals around home.
We never had a cow.
Once in a while
    we'd raise a pig.
My aunts and uncles, everybody had cattle around us,
    so we always had fresh milk and butter, that kind of thing.

We kept chickens penned up,
    that were laying hens,
    and we had big white and red chickens we kept for laying hens.
And then we had banty chickens and game chickens that ran free.
And then we had geese and ducks and guineas and turkeys and all,
    any kind of farm fowl that you could imagine.
And we also had a bunch of dogs, cats,
    and usually a bunch of wild pets, too,
        you know, possums and skunks and crows and different kinds of
            stuff
      that we'd carry home.
And everyone walked, too, when I was young.
And it wasn't anything to walk from my aunt's house in Big Witch
    down to our house in Cherokee,   .
    a six- or eight-mile walk.
And that was just one direction, you know,
    then you had to walk back home once you got through visiting.
And yet everybody did it,
    nobody thought anything about it.
They say the community really changed
    when they put Highway 19 in across Soco Mountain.
Then when the national park was developed,
    that was another tremendous change in this community.
And with the park dedication came the tourist industry,
    and the whole economy changed.
You know, it went from an agricultural community
    dependent on farming and logging for economic stability,
    it went to an industry focused on catering to the tourists.
And today, let's see, 90 to 95 percent of the business in this town
    is tourist oriented.
And it's been a kind of a double-edged sword, in a lot of ways.
We have a tremendous renaissance in our arts,
    because people can market their work now   ·
    and make a living at this.
And so, you know, a lot of traditions have been kept alive
    because of the tourist industry.
On the other hand,
    we have all the development that goes along with it,

the pollution,
and the demographics of millions of people coming through
　　　　your town
in a summer season.
Things like this
　　that really impact the environment,
　　change the attitude of the individual in a community
　　toward how they should live and what they should do.
Growing up
　　I thought the best job in town was chiefing,
　　get to stand there in the sun all day
　　and have your picture made with pretty girls.
I thought,
　　"This is the way to make a living."
And it is a lucrative occupation,
　　even though it promotes the stereotype
　　of all Indians being feather-wearing, pony-riding, tipi-living
　　　　people.
Since *Dances with Wolves* and *Last of the Mohicans*
　　and different movies like that,
　　the stereotype is beginning to change;
　　it's still there, but
　　they're starting to accept someone who isn't wearing a war
　　　　bonnet
　　as an Indian.

❯❯ Jeannie and the Booger

When I was growing up,
　　with all my cousins,
　　the old outhouse was something.
There's a lot of funny stories about that.
One time we,

and like I said, we had a lot of chickens that just ran free.
A rooster had gotten down in the hole in the outhouse,
　　and it couldn't fly out,
　　its wings were too wide to come out of the hole.

And my cousin had gone and sat down in the outhouse,
    and when she turned the lights out on the rooster,
    the rooster went crazy,
    and it scared her.
And here she came
    with her britches down around her legs,
    just screaming like crazy,
    down the middle of the garden.
She was only about six or eight years old, too.
She just knew a booger had got her.

➤ Grandpa and Grandma

My grandmother always felt that we should assimilate
    and become part of mainstream America.
So the Baptist religion, minding your manners, being dressed
        properly
    and having good manners,
    being able to conduct yourself in public or at home in a proper
        manner,
    was something that my grandmother really focused on.
And that was totally opposite of what my grandfather liked to do.
You know he made moonshine most of his life,
    he liked to fish and hunt,
    so I feel like I had kinda the best of both worlds growing up.
My grandfather always had me on the mountain
    or down at the creek into some kind of meanness,
    and my grandmother was always teaching me the right way,
    or the way to be accepted in any culture.
She told us to "act like somebody."
And something else that I heard,
    probably on an everyday basis,
    was that you can do anything you want to, you know,
    as long as you don't offend anyone,
    and as long as that's what you want to do.
No matter what it is or how hard it is, you know,
    there's a way to do it
    if you really want to do it.

And that's something I've always thought, too,
    that I've always been able to do anything,
    and have done,
    just about anything I've always wanted to.
And there's something else—
    I didn't hear "No"
    as much as I heard "You could do it this way
    instead of that way."
They tried to give you an alternative instead of a denial.
This was something that,
    I think,
    got the work done without a lot of fuss, in the parents' view,
    and it also taught a lesson.
That's how I grew up.
I had thirty-two first cousins,
    and most of them grew up in Cherokee.
And I knew—
    all my aunts and uncles were around,
    my dad didn't have any brothers and sisters, he was an only
        child,
    but Mom is one of six, she has three sisters and two brothers,
    and they all had family.
I had four cousins that were almost the same age I was.
All four girls, Mom and her three sisters,
    all had children all at the same time.
We were all within like about five or six months of one another.
So we all grew up together.
And growing up with my cousins was
    just like growing up with your brothers and sisters, we were just
        as close,
    and the responsibility of watching after the children
    and disciplining the children was shared by the adults.
You'd catch another child doing something and take it to their
    parent for punishment.
You punished them right then—
    is the way they looked at it.
And if one was punished,
    everybody usually got punished.

So it was a good life growing up.
We lived in what would be considered a shack now,
   but it was one of the best houses on the road
   when I was growing up.
There was about five houses on the road that I grew up on,
   and now there's about fifty,
   so within a thirty-year time period,
   that's the kind of development we've experienced in this
      community.
That's why I say
   everybody now has their own house.
And extended family really doesn't have a chance now,
   the way it used to.
In the past everybody had to live together
   because there wasn't anywhere else to live.
It was a, I imagine,
   it was a really poor community in this part of the country
   at one time,
   but nobody needed much.
If you don't need much,
   you don't want much, I guess.
Or vice versa,
   if you don't want much,
   you don't need a whole lot.
Most everybody that I knew growing up was happy.
You didn't hear about mental illness and depression.
And everybody drank, you know, and stuff,
   but you didn't hear about alcoholism being a destructive
      element in families.
I know all the men in our family drank,
   but they didn't drink at Granny's house.
She didn't allow any drinking and any card playing,
   or nothing like that around her.
But my great uncle, her brother,
   and my great-great-uncle lived in the house right below us,
   and they always drank,
   and had fighting roosters,
   and traded horses,

and there was always a crowd like that around.
There wasn't any fighting and shooting
   and all this stuff that's associated with drinking
   that happens in the community today.
And the attitude was completely different.
The people that drink and carry on now
   don't have any respect for anything, not even themselves, you
       know.
And these people that I grew up around—
   hard-working people, they put in a day's work.
When they built Frontierland over here,
   my uncle leased part of that property to the amusement park,
   and one of our neighbors,
   a fellow named Kemp Sneed—
      well, shoot, he was related to us, too,
      my Aunt Mindy was my grandmother's aunt,
      his father and she were sisters—
   so Uncle Kemp came out and told Uncle Tom,
   he said,
   "Well Tom," he said,
   "now that you're gettin' this lease money off of this land down
      here,
   I guess you'll stay drunk all the time, won't you?"
Uncle Tom said,
   "Hell, I stay drunk all the time anyway."
He said,
   "Now I'll just drink better liquor."
But there was always that kind of camaraderie,
   and joking and carrying on.
Nobody had their feelings hurt.
Once in a while there was,
  I've heard about violence in the community,
   but it wasn't usually associated with drinking, and things like
      that,
   not like it is today.
And the fights around the ball games used to be something
   that the non-Indian community really had a hard time dealing
      with here.

And eventually
    gambling associated with the ball games was outlawed.
And the only way that they were able to change the attitude of the
        ball players
    and the community
    was to start paying the ball players to play ball as an exhibition
    instead of as a match to win a prize.
And so the government and the agency here,
    and probably the police force and, you know,
    the entities that control the community
    got together
    and through trial and error, I'm sure,
    devised this way.
And today when we have ball games,
    each ball player gets a fee for playing the game,
    and so the violence and roughness and stuff like that
    aren't as bad as they used to be.
There are still ways of working out disagreements in a ball game,
        you know,
    kind of like there used to be.
There's no betting on the sidelines now,
    and used to,
    people on both sides would bring all kinds of stuff
    like money, and canned goods, and clothes, and shoes,
        everything.
They'd pile all this up
    down on the end of the field, on a big sheet or a big blanket,
    and the winning team got to divide that up.
And they said
    a lot of the fights on the sideline
    were between women whose men were fighting on the ball
        field.
At that time,
    the teams would be from different communities.
[Each community used to represent a clan.]
The clan system has almost completely died out.
Now there's people that can trace their clan,
    but because of a lot of intermarriage,

and because of some clans being almost completely wiped out
    with the epidemics and things like that,
      the clan system really died out.
Christianity, too,
    with the idea of the woman marrying into the man's family,
    was another issue that broke the clan system down.
Still, if you go to someone for traditional medicine,
    a lot of times they'll want to know what your clan is,
    or who your grandmother belonged to,
    you know, what clan she was from.
And I'm sure that some of the formulas and prayers relate directly
        to certain clans,
    and clan members and their association with the culture.
Because some clans were,
    well, I get the idea that they had specific duties within the
        culture,
    but I've never read anything about this,
    I've never heard that there was a hierarchy among the clans.
They were numbered,
    because the women, depending on their clan,
    wore a certain number of shells on their leg when they danced.
I've heard that,
    so that they were identified by color and number,
    but I don't think that there was a whole lot of significance
        between the clans.
I think some may have been a lot larger than others,
    and this may have dictated some authority of some sort,
    but you know so much of that kind of history was lost—
    because it was oral history and never recorded—
    that now it's almost entirely speculation.
You know, I read a lot of things that were documented,
    but a lot of times I've heard the story somewhere else,
    and the literature that I read—
    it's only part of what I've heard.
So like I say,
    now you know,
    a lot of people consider what's been recorded as the whole truth.
    but it's only bits and pieces.

It's kind of like the Bible,
    a lot of people like to take scripture out of context,
    a passage,
    and a lot of people do that with our history.
They'll take an event and exploit it one way or another,
    to get what they want out of it.
I see that happen,
    happening a lot today.
You know—
    it's always happened, I suppose,
    I don't guess there's any way around it.
Storytelling, as a traditional art form, is, you know,
    like I say,
    today, is something people really preserve by researching
    and understanding these stories so that they can retell them.
Instead of passing on a part of the history
    that they know has to be conveyed this way
    so that it will continue to exist.
It used to be
    they told a lot of the education stories,
    about who their family was and what they'd done,
    historical events that maybe someone in the family had been
        part of,
    things like that would a lot of times come out.
Even through like fishing and hunting stories,
    stories about something funny that happened at the grocery
        store,
    something like that, you know.
And way back when my grandparents were growing up,
    there was a lot of transition from season to season,
    and what was going on.
Preparation for planting gardens
    and getting ready for the summer,
    this time of year was always a big event.
Everybody had to really work hard this time of year.
When the crops were planted,
    after they got up and going good,
    I think they had a lot of leisure time

until it was time to start harvesting the crops,
and then it went back to work time.
And then in the dead of winter, I think,
they had some time.
There were a lot of things that were done as daily chores,
but there wasn't a whole lot of extra work that needed to be done,
not unless it was associated with the care of the livestock or
something like that.
Once they got the garden in and all their canning done,
usually by Thanksgiving, you know,
the hogs had been slaughtered,
everything had been gotten ready for winter.
That time I think was spent a lot on—
I know the women used to have sewing clubs,
you know, they'd come together and make quilts.
I can remember that kind of thing going on in the wintertime
around home.
And hunting was always big in the winter,
used to hunt and trap a lot in the wintertime.
So from season to season
the activities pretty much differed.
And you always had daily chores,
like my job was to carry water, I'd fill the reservoir up.
We cooked and heated with wood.
We had a reservoir on the end of the wood cookstove,
where you held about five gallons of water,
I'd have to fill that up every day.
Then we had two big two-and-a-half-gallon water buckets
that I would have to keep filled on the wash bench
out on the porch.
And that moved in the house in the wintertime.
The Green Corn Ceremony
was something that took place after the corn had gotten ripe,
in the summertime,
and I think there in those times, when people had some leisure
time,
and different things like that came about,
there was a lot of feasting and ceremony.

I've never seen the ceremony, the dance.
You know, Walker Calhoun and those guys at Big Cove
    are performing some of those ceremonies nowdays.
But I've never seen the Green Corn Dance done as a ceremony.
I've seen the dance in the Unto These Hills drama, you know,
    but that's been choreographed for the production.
That was, I think,
    a time when there was a realization of
    another year of existence for the tribe,
    because corn was such a vital part of the diet, you know.
Even in recent years,
    when this community was still an agricultural community,
    corn was very important.
You know,
    you used it for the meal to make your bread,
    you ate the roasting ears,
    you put it up,
    you pickled corn,
    you know,
    so it was a food supply for the people as well as the livestock.
We always had big fields of corn for the hogs and cattle and horses.
Tobacco is something too
    that was raised as a commercial crop
    by our family when I was growing up.
I saw some benefit from it in the long run,
    you know, through clothes and food on the table, and stuff like
        that,
    but to me at the time it was a lot of free labor—
    I spent a lot of days in the tobacco field.
I remember Grandpa making plugs of tobacco, twists,
    out of the sucker leavers that came off the stalks,
    after the tobacco had been cut.
There's a couple-three little leaves that'll come back out on the stalk
    at the bottom after they cut it.
We put the tobacco up lot of times.
He would take the hands and cure 'em and make twists to chew,
    and he always had commercial tobacco to smoke.
Everybody in my family smoked.

I think I developed some complex toward tobacco
    when I had to work it as a child.
I've never chewed or smoked or anything.
But all my family did, and,
    but they always smoked commercial cigarettes and tobacco.
I remember my Uncle Pete and my grandpa rolling their own
        cigarettes
    out of like Prince Albert and Bull Durham,
    and that was something that has died out in this community too,
    is a lot of the little intricacies of that habit, you know,
    smoking and rolling your own tobacco.
I can remember seeing my grandfather lay a cigarette paper in his
        hand,
    and he'd put tobacco on it, and put his hands together,
    and kind of roll 'em as he turned 'em over,
    and have a cigarette rolled.
Just, and it looked to me,
    there may have been more to it than what I thought he was
        doing,
    it looked like he just kind of rolled his hand over
    and kind of pulled his hands when he did it,
    and just rolled a cigarette right up.
I wonder a lot of times
    if some of my lung problems aren't associated with second-hand
        smoke
    growing up, cause everybody smoked.
Mom said she started smoking as soon as she was old enough to
        hold a cigarette.
They thought it was cute to let her smoke, you know.
This past year she had to have heart surgery,
    and they tried to get her to quit smoking,
    and she still smokes just like a freight train.
The story that I've heard a lot about the origin of tobacco,
    is that it sprouted and grew
    where the first man and woman made love
    and was a sacred plant
    to be used for purification and for fertility.
Purification is what I've seen it used for more than anything.

And there's Indian tobacco, Cherokee tobacco,
    there's a few people around that still raise it,
    or used to, I don't know whether they still do or not.
Once in a while you can get a-hold of some of it.
You know, and there's sweats and different ceremonies—
    a lot of times like when the dance grounds were blessed,
    tobacco was used.
For prosperity, you know,
    tobacco is used a lot of times and just considered a sacred thing.
You know pleasure smoking, I think, was something where
    they took tobacco totally out of context,
    and it was addictive if you smoked a lot of it,
    you know the nicotine is addictive.
But you know the Cherokees had so many plants
    and formulas for different combinations of plants,
    and so many alternatives to smoking tobacco,
    that they didn't do that a lot, I don't think.
Now when I was growing up
    I can remember going to a lot of old peoples' homes,
    and usually after a meal,
    the women would smoke a pipe.
I knew a lot of old Indian women that kept one of them little bitty
        pipes,
    some of them were made out of wood,
    some of them were those stone pipes or little clay pipes,
    once in a while you'd see somebody with a commercial tobacco
        pipe.
Most of the time they were just little old homemade pipes
    with a piece of cane or something stuck in for a stem.
They'd just take 'em two or three little puffs of tobacco, you know,
    and that'd be about it.
My grandmother always smoked cigarettes, Mom, my aunts,
    everybody when they'd come to the house,
    you know, everybody was smoking cigarettes.
We used to harvest ginseng, you know, dig it, sell it,
    and I use it quite a bit.
It's real good for like an upset stomach,

if you get kind of a sour stomach,
    just chew a piece of it and swallow the juice off of it,
    and it's bitter, it's just bitter as gall.
That's what I use it for.
It brings a pretty good price now,
    you know, like from sixty to a hundred and sixty dollars a pound
        now,
    depending on who you sell it to and what size the roots are
    and things like that.
Yeah, that was something that we always did
    to kind of supplement the income in the fall of the year,
That was usually where I got my new boots,
    we'd dig enough ginseng to buy a pair of boots.
I didn't ever get to sell the 'seng,
    I'd always put it with Grandpa's, you know, but he'd sell it.
There used to be a store up here on Highway 19,
    going up Soco,
    always called it White Trees,
    there's still a White Tree Motel right there,
    but they sold some clothes and shoes and stuff,
    and sold Wolverine work boots.
And that's the kind of boots I'd buy every fall,
    I'd get a new pair of boots about every fall.
And usually in the spring, too,
    I'd have 'em wore out by the spring,
    use my old boots to fish in
    and get me a new pair to work in.
Some of the old people chewed ginseng.
Now I know different people'll carry a piece in their pocket, you
        know,
    they'll use it like that,
    but I don't think they use it,
    it's not a real widespread thing.
I think that's probably the use of—
    what's referred to now as holistic medicine
    or "medicine"—
    is something that has really kind of died out of the community.

There's a lot of people who used to work as midwives and as herb
        doctors,
    don't have any clientele any more,
    and it's the modern hospital.
And modern medicine's so convenient
    that people would rather take a pill
    than prepare a recipe for a poultice
    or something like that, you know,
    all in the interest of conserving time.
I think people are interested in it,
    but,
    just like the storytelling,
    the interest is only strong enough in a few people
    for them to really research it,
    and have it become a part of them
    to where that they understand it enough to use it.
It's kind of like gathering mushrooms, you know,
    it's really difficult for a lot of young people
    to spend enough time in the woods
    to understand which ones to pick.
And it's—there's quite a few people, though,
    that are taking a real sincere interest in stuff like that.
A lot of people, once they learn, they kind of convert,
    start using that really more than modern medicine.
There's a lot of preventive medicine
    and wild medicine
    that you can't find in modern medicine.
Comfrey's a great preventive medicine,
    you can use that stuff for anything.
And I use a lot of yellowroot for an astringent,
    it's good for cuts and stuff like that,
    as a wash kind of like witch hazel,
    and it's good for ulcers in the stomach,
    intestinal problems.
I use it for sore mouth or, you know,
    something like that.
It's not strong enough to cure an abscess or anything like that,

I don't know of any antibiotics that we have here
   that would be strong enough for a severe infection like that.
And they claim a long time ago
   that a lot of Native Americans died from abscessed teeth.
Because of the unglazed pottery, they had a lot of grit in their food,
   and because they used their teeth for tools, it wore them down.
A lot of people would live a long time if they could live through the
            years,
   their thirties and forties, when they lost their teeth.
That dramatically figures into the statistics of mortality among
            Native Americans.
When you look at it, they can tell by the,
   I guess it deforms the jaw when you get an abscess or severe
            infection like that,
   to the point where it sets up gangrene.
So they can tell that's what killed them.
Toothache killed them.
I wonder a lot of times if that's why our foods were made up
   so much of soups and stews.
You know, just about all of our food was a one-pot recipe—
   had to prepare their foods that way just to be able to eat it.
It's a lot easier to eat a boiled rabbit than a roasted rabbit.
A lot of that kind of thinking is just my own theories.
You know it all figured in, though,
   in the big scheme of things,
      it's bound to.

Grandpa made whiskey out of just about anything.
He made a lot of homemade wines, made brandies, a lot of just
            corn liquor.
The beer that they made, to make the liquor from, too, they'd drink
            a lot of times.
He told a story once
   about making about four sixty-gallon barrels of this beer
   to make liquor out of it.
They lived on Kirkland's Creek—
   that's about halfway between here and Bryson City,

they had an old logging camp up there,
    had a house up there, and they stayed out there and logged all
        the time.
But he and Uncle Tom were down there,
    and he said it was just them two had been there,
    and he said the beer worked off and got fermented.
He said
    they decided they'd drink some of it
    before they started making it into whiskey.
He said they went and got a water bucket full of it
    and just started drinking it out of a dipper.
He said after the first bucket,
    he said that they was both feeling real good.
He said after the second bucket,
    neither one of them could make it to the third bucket.
But he said they drank a whole barrel of that stuff in about a week.
So they must have just been dog drunk for a week there.
I don't know whether anybody come up to help them or not.
He said that stuff would really get you going.

One time
    he'd made a bunch of wine out of elderberries,
    and hadn't let it work off completely before he jarred it up,
    and put it in Mason jars.
And my grandmother was sitting on the steps
    out in the front of the house one evening,
    shelling beans,
    and the sun got down low enough
    to where it started shining in between the steps and hitting those
        jars,
    and one of the jars blew up
    and just caused a chain reaction in that box full of jars.
She throwed green beans all over the front yard
    trying to get away from it.
I bet Grandpa was in bad trouble then.
He was gone when that happened.
I was gone when he got home,
    so I don't know really what took place

when Granny finally caught up with him.
It must have been something,
    cause he wasn't supposed to have anything like that around the
        house at all.

In my family
    the women are usually the ones who make the important
        decisions,
    and usually the ones who ensure
    that the family's economy is what it should be.
They pay the bills,
    and take care of the domestic business, you know.
And my mother and my Aunt Sally and Aunt Alta,
    they always were really strong and independent.
My grandfather was always gone,
    and they had to be that way.
They'd say Grandpa'd leave going fishing
    and might not come back for two or three years.
She said one time he left and was going after a loaf of bread,
    and said it was a couple years before he came back.
And when he came back,
    he came back and had a loaf of bread, and said,
    throwed it on the table just like he'd been down to the store.
And she'd always take him back.
But he worked all over the country, did a lot of construction work,
    cleared right of way, he and my uncle.
One time
    they were arrested and didn't have any identification on them,
    and they thought they were illegal immigrants,
    getting ready to send them back to Mexico,
    and Grandpa said, "I couldn't even speak Mexican."
They were something.
People that worked away from here with my grandfather and my
        uncles
    said that they were always men to drink,
    that Grandpa would always get something started.
And my Uncle Pete was a big man, pretty mean.
And he said my Uncle Pete would just knock about a half a dozen out,

to get him out of the trouble he'd get started.
I bet they were something else
    when they were young men and could get around good.
And my Uncle Pete's dead now,
    my grandpa's lived to be eighty-five.
He's still getting around pretty good,
    he's still got a pretty good memory,
    he still talks about a lot of things that happened.
My grandpa was born in 1909,
    and my grandmother was born in 1906.
She was just a little bit older than he was.
They went through a lot.
Granny was raised by her aunt and uncle too,
    her parents passed away when she was fairly young.
They had one of the more progressive farms around.
Uncle Tom was always trading horses,
    had money, and he was always wheeling and dealing,
    and they had a good wagon and a good barn.
Granny said they always had a lot of excess food.
She said sometimes Aunt Lizzie and Uncle Tom
    would load up a wagonload full of goods,
    and take off out through the community and
    checking on people that needed stuff.
Aunt Lizzie was kind of a doctor and a midwife.
People would come over and stay at the house a lot,
    and Granny said a lot of times on Sunday they'd feed forty or fifty
        people,
    Sunday evening.
She said they always had a lot of food, though.
They'd like pickle in big barrels and put everything up in huge
        amounts.
She said Aunt Lizzie didn't can in quart jars,
    she'd can in half-gallon and gallon jars.
She said until she got about five hundred to a thousand jars in the
        cellar,
    she wasn't happy.
But she said every year when they got ready to can again,
    everything was poured out.

Everything was new every year.
I've done that a lot of days, washed jars and emptied jars.
Used to have a big old black pot that Granny'd build a fire under.
I remember washing clothes in it when I was real young,
    but they had an old wringer washing machine too.
Sometimes I think that I'm kind of right on the edge,
    I was able to experience just a little bit of that before it died.
It didn't really die I don't think,
    it was just kind of replaced with a lot of things.
A lot of that attitude,
    and that kind of respect for that kind of lifestyle
    will always be around
    for some people, you know.
The majority's been overwhelmed by modern convenience,
    and distractions,
    all this other stuff we've got going on today.
There's just a lot of change happening right now,
    and I think that it's good, we needed change, you know.
And how this change is looked at by our politicians
    and used by the people
    will be something that will be really important in the next eight
        or ten years.
I don't think that we can really say what's going to happen right
        now.
We've got issues like the gaming,
    and issues of sovereignty,
    and issues of just being federally recognized,
    these state tribes and things like that, a lot of issues.
The gambling's gonna be an issue that kind of makes or breaks us.
I'm afraid what might happen is
    that we'll become independent of a lot of government money
    that we've been guaranteed through treaties in the past.
And we'll become independent of that because of the gaming
        money.
Then if they ever took gaming away from us—
If they ever do away with the reservation here,
    if the land's ever taken out of trust of the federal government,
    then soon after that

I feel
this tribe would be separated
and they'll just dissolve into mainstream America.
On the other hand
if we can get some leaders who are interested in tribal welfare
instead of their own welfare,
I think that they'll develop foundations and mechanisms
so that we can continue to be an independent tribe.

Edna Chekelelee

When I remember Edna, I smell woodsmoke and fry bread, I feel her big, warm hug, I see her eyes twinkling as she joked with her husband, Boyd, and I hope that she is happy in a heaven that includes both "Christians and buffaloes," as a friend of hers suggested. Edna passed away in 1995 at the age of sixty-five. She grew up speaking Cherokee in a very traditional family in the Snowbird community, part of the Qualla Boundary lands located in Graham County, North Carolina. She was Wolf Clan, and she claimed Junaluska as her great-grandfather's brother. Edna worked with other people in the Snowbird community to clean up the area around Junaluska's grave in Robbinsville, to put up a fence and keep the area neat.

But Edna's real work was with children and young people. Although she didn't physically give birth to any babies, she adopted seven children and raised them—and then raised many more, taking in babies and teenagers alike. Even when they were all grown, Edna still worried about them, prayed for them, and helped them in any way she could.

Throughout her life she taught young people about their Cherokee heritage: she taught them what it meant to be Cherokee, and she taught them to be proud of it. She taught Cherokee language, which she spoke in the western dialect because of having grown up in Snowbird. She taught arts and crafts; she taught traditional Cherokee dances and led a young people's dance group for years; she sang with her mother and with several gospel groups; and every year, beginning in 1976, she hosted a three-day singing at her house and grounds, with music by white and Cherokee gospel groups from the mountains of North Carolina and from Oklahoma. A devout Christian, Edna also believed strongly in traditional Cherokee medicine and was comfortable with combining these beliefs. She used to sing "Oh, How I Love Jesus" and "Amazing Grace" in the sweat lodge.

Edna learned to tell stories, weave baskets, and use plants for medicine growing up with her extended family in the Snowbird Community. She loved to sit on the front porch in the evenings with the elders, listening to them tell stories. "At that time it didn't sink in, but the more I think about it the more it comes back to me." She doesn't remember how she started telling stories herself, but she has told stories to her children, extended family, and friends, as well as performing in public.

She finished high school, married her husband, Boyd, and was teaching about Cherokee culture in whatever ways she could for many years before it became as accepted as it is today. She always loved to travel. When I met Edna in 1983, she was traveling to folk festivals, school programs, and powwows throughout the region. She taught part-time in the arts and crafts program of the Graham County Schools so that she could teach the many Cherokee children in that school system about Cherokee culture.

➤➤

Edna knew many traditional stories about animals and about origins. Later in her life, when these stories were collected, she was developing a storytelling style that combined history, stories, personal experience, and humor. When Edna told stories, she also taught her audience to speak Cherokee; she drummed, sang, danced, and used props like the Trail of Tears basket and the cross in a hoop. In her storytelling, as in her life, all of Cherokee culture was an integrated whole.

One of her stories says that the Indian people knew about Jesus before Columbus arrived. Other Cherokee people tell stories, not included here, describing how the Little People brought the news of Jesus to the Cherokee, how they came and told the Cherokee when Jesus was born and then told about his life and his crucifixion.

When the Cherokee Little People heard about Jesus' death, they wept, and wherever their tears fell to the ground, they turned into "fairy crosses"—the unusual cross-shaped gems found in the southern Appalachians.

Other stories, such as "The Trees Are Alive," "The Deer," "Mother Earth's Spring Dress," and "The Quail Dance," reveal traditional Cherokee values relating to the earth. Several of Edna's stories concern the Removal and the Trail of Tears: "The Legend of the Corn Beads," "Elders on the Mountains," and "The Trail of Tears Basket." Another story, "The Indian Preacher," was told especially for a Cherokee audience and is a classic humorous anecdote. Two of the tales collected here come from personal experience. "Santeetlah Ghost Story" is a personal story with a positive moral ending that I first heard Edna tell to elementary school children at Halloween. "Feathers" is a personal story about American Indian identity that uses humor to describe an encounter with the dominant culture's stereotypes. Many Cherokee people tell similar humorous stories about others' misconceptions of their identity.

Edna's storytelling was an important part of her life, just as storytelling is an important part of Cherokee culture. Edna used stories to entertain her children and to teach them (and anyone else who was around) how to act, to teach outsiders about Cherokee culture, and to teach Cherokee history and philosophy to audiences throughout the Southeast. Although I listened to Edna's stories at many different events over the twelve years that I knew her, the stories in this book were collected on three separate occasions. One was a public performance given as part of the Sisters of the South Tour, sponsored by the Southern Arts Federation. This performance included "Cherokee Language," "The Trees Are Alive," "Mother Earth's Spring Dress," "The Deer," and "Jesus before Columbus Time." Two stories, "The Legend of the Corn Beads" and "Santeetlah Ghost Story," were taken from a videotaped interview session. The third event was a small gathering at the Qualla Arts and Crafts Co-op of members of the newly formed speakers' bureau, Kekasuyeta. During this evening, about twenty Cherokee people shared their knowledge of history, stories, medicine, and culture as a way of starting off the speakers' bureau. It was a special evening in which people affirmed their culture and their identity with laughter, stories, and shared emotions.

Edna told "Storytelling," "Elders on the Mountains," "The Quail Dance," "Feathers," "The Indian Preacher," and "The Trail of Tears Basket." None of Edna's stories are found in Mooney's collection.

›› Cherokee Language

Repeat after me,   Siyo.
A little louder   Siyo.
You said "Hello."
Osigwugah   osigwugah.
You said "How are you?"
Osigwuh   osigwuh.
All right [laughter].
Now, you learned my language.

I learned your language when I was five years old.
I had to, regardless if I wanted to or not.
When I went to school we were told that we had to learn
    one way or another
If I didn't learn I had to go to the bathroom,
    wash my mouth out with Ivory soap.
But I never did wash my Indian language out,
    I still got it in my heart,
    and I still carry on my Indian language.

›› The Trees Are Alive

One time I was praying in Cherokee,
    somebody said,
    "How come you're praying for the trees?"
I said,
    "Cause they're alive.
    Without trees we couldn't make it.
    We wouldn't have no shade
    and feel this clean air."
And I said,
    "That's why
    I always pray for the creatures

and the trees
  'cause God made us."
And somebody said,
  "Well, He didn't make the tree."
I said,
  "Don't make a mistake,
  He did make the tree.
  He made life, water, and trees."

›› Mother Earth's Spring Dress

And this time of year
  our Mother Earth has worked all winter long
  in making her dress,
  beautiful dress,
  but it's green.
'Bout the early spring she adds some flowers to it.
And whenever she gets ready
  she drops her skirt down the mountainside,
  you can see it across the mountain
  downhill,
  all her skirt is full
  with all the flowers—
  dogwood flowers, azaleas,
  and all kinds of flowers.
That's our Mother's skirt
  that she had worked on all winter long.
So rejoice in it
  and try to keep it clean—
  this is our Mother Earth that we walk on.

›› The Deer

When we kill the deer—
  our men kill deer—
  they don't waste any kinds of bones or antlers or the meat;
  they share the meat.
Back a long time ago the village would be like this—

they shared their meat with one other,
and we don't do that as much anymore.
Whenever we have bones,
they saved the bones for the knitting, for the crocheting,
and used all parts of the deer,
it's not wasted.
And when they go hunting,
they only get one,
they don't get all the deer out there.
And they save it for the next person.

➤➤ Jesus before Columbus Time

Before the Columbus time
we lived in log houses,
we never did live in tipis.
And on each end of the Indian village
where we lived would be—
one of these crosses
would sit on each corner of the village,
and it's much bigger than this.
I carry this to show you what I'm talking about.
This is a circle meaning four corners of the world.
We live, we're sitting on four corners of the world.
And right in the middle is the cross where Jesus died.
And Columbus came, he said,
    "What's that?"
We said,
    "Well, this is what represents what we believe in.
    What was our hearts.
    And this is where Jesus died on the cross."
And each color represents something.
Red is purest blood, and that's east and means success.
And white is peace—
    Jesus has made peace for us where it was rough before,
    and we got punished before.
    Nowadays it's so much easier:
    all we have to do is believe in him in our hearts

as we walk "close to Thee."
Red—east, white—south,
   and west is black—and honor the dead.
And the north is blue.
And green,
   green is our Mother Earth which we walk on.
When you're walking on the Mother Earth and see trash,
   pick it up,
   keep your Mother Earth clean,
   by doing that you keep her clean.
All right, we go on down, and this is yellow, which is sunrise,
   and someday we're going to see sunrise
   and God's son will be coming.
So I thought we'd pass that on.
And Columbus say, "How did you know that?"
We always knew it;
   we knew that God was in our hearts,
   and He always told us what was right and wrong.
When we go and do something wrong,
   we always knew it was going to be wrong,
   so we always have to keep our heart clean
   by believing in Him
   and as He died for us, for our sins.

❯❯ The Legend of the Corn Beads

Cherokee women
   wear the legendary necklace made of corn beads.
It is a gift
   from the Great Spirit
   in the shape of a teardrop.
This is the Cherokee legend of the corn beads.
In the 1800s
   during the Trail of Tears,
   the corn stalks were eight feet tall,
   and corn was twelve to eighteen inches long.
The corn stood back and watched
   as the Indian people were getting pushed and shoved

by the white soldiers.
And the corn cried and cried.
And the teardrop landed on the corn fodder,
    and the corn dropped down to three feet tall.
That's why it's called teardrop,
    our mother of corn.
The Cherokee women used these teardrops,
    our mother of corn,
    to make beautiful cornbeads,
    but to me this is sad.
But it is a way to remember
    the Trail of Tears.

›› **Santeetlah Ghost Story**

I was born
    back in Santeetlah, where Joyce Kilmer is now.
And we used to walk
    from there to school to Snowbird,
    and we walked to go to church,
    somewhere about fourteen mile round-trip.
Anyway, a long walk,
    and sometimes we'd be barefooted
    even in wintertime.
Sometimes we didn't have good clothes to wear.
Now we are lucky that we got clothes flying all over the place.
And they're abusing our clothes,
    and I feel sorry for the good clothes that's in trash cans—
    we wish we had that whenever we was growing up.
But this is a ghost story.
Somebody had passed away,
    and my daddy said we had to go set up,
    'cause they believed in setting up all night;
    when somebody died,
    one of their relatives,
    they'd set up all night long,
    they wouldn't sleep.
So he said, "We're going to have to go."

So we left,
    I think it was right around eight o'clock in the evening.
When we got the news, it was seven,
    so it was eight o'clock, probably, when we got ready to go.
So we crossed the river,
    and we had big rocks that we jumped over
    to get across,
    so we crossed over,
    and we started climbing up the hill.
And nothing but laurel bush and moonlight,
    that's all we could see,
    going up the trail.
So we walked the trail, and I was behind my mother,
    and she was walking in front of me,
    and then I grabbed her skirt and hang on to it
    'cause I was always afraid of the dark.
'Cause I used to listen to the old people
    sit out on the porch;
    they leaned back on their chairs
    and they spit their tobacco wa-a-ay out.
And when they spit tobacco,
    then
    they was ready to tell stories.
So I would listen.
They would tell some ghost stories,
    and there was one ghost story I was always afraid of,
    and thought, sure enough, there must be ghosts.
So we was walking on the trail,
    and as we walked up
    I heard something going like this: [whistling sound].
And I said,
    "Daddy, what is it?"
And he said,
    "Oh, don't worry about it, everything's okay."
And I keep hearing it getting closer.
I said,
    "Daddy, it's getting closer, what is it?"
It would go like [rhythmic whistle],

like that,
    so it must have been a-breathing,
    that sound that I heard.
Anyway, I got close to my mother, and I closed my eyes,
    and I kept hearing something behind me.
Then I got between my mother and dad,
    in the middle,
    and I closed my eyes tighter.
And then finally I peeped a little bit,
    and I saw something white behind me.
And as we walked up, Daddy said,
    "Everything's going to be all right.
    Don't get scared.
    You don't ever get scared.
    If you don't get scared, everything'll be okay."
So—I couldn't help but shake.
But I thought I would just keep walking.
Finally Daddy said,
    "Okay, everybody stop.
    Get back up on the side.
    Let that thing go through
    in front of us."
I said,
    "What is it?"
He said,
    "Oh, that's okay, I'll take care of it."
So we stood back on the side,
    on a bank,
    and I kept hearing
    chomping on the leaves,
    and it would go
    [heavy breathing] like that.
And I peeped,
    opened my eyes like that,
    and I saw nothing but a
        sheer
        white
        cloth

looked like a clinging curtain,
   and it didn't have no head,
   no shape over the head,
   all I saw was the shoulders.
So he was standing right on the side,
   and Daddy said,
   "All right."
He said,
   "You've scared my children enough,"
   said, "I just about know who you are,"
   said, "go on ahead and step ahead,
   I don't care about you."
Said,
   "Go on ahead, and step ahead.
   You're not going to hurt my children,
   and I'm not going to hurt you.
   Just go on by, we made room for you to go by."
And all at once we heard a little bit,
   and it just chompin' up the leaves.
All at once I closed my eyes again,
   and I kept hearing—
   and I just shook.
Finally I opened my eyes
   a little bit like that,
   and here he was going up in the air—
   no feet,
   and all I could see was sheer cloth
   climbing up the laurel bushes like that.
And finally just went on
   through the laurel bushes,
   and it faded away.
And Daddy said,
   "He's gone, he left us alone, so don't worry about it.
   Don't ever get scared, everything'll be okay."
So ever since then I felt much better about being in the dark.
I'm still afraid of the dark [laughs].
But just remember, if you're not afraid,
   a ghost can't hurt you.

If you get afraid and panic,
>you might run over a cliff or fall and hurt yourself.
But if you're not afraid,
>a ghost can't hurt you.

›› **Storytelling**

My name is Edna Chekelelee.
I was born and raised in Santeetlah,
>and I used to sit around with the old people
>that sit around and talk.
They'd lean back with their chairs,
>and they'd spit their tobacco
>w-a-a-y out.
And they would say,
>"Shoo, go in the other room, go play with your little sister."
I'd say,
>"I don't want to play with them."
They'd say,
>"Shoo, go play."
I'd say,
>"I don't want to play with them."
They'd say,
>"Go on, you don't need to listen to this mean talk with the elder
>>people.
>It's mean talk. You don't need to hear it."
I said okay.
So I walked off the porch,
>I'd go around behind the end of the porch,
>then I'd crawl back up on the porch,
>and I'd get behind the chairs where they were leaning back—
>sort of made a place where I could crawl back—
>so then I laid down,
>and I listened what they were saying.
At that time
>it didn't sink in,
>but the more I think about it
>the more it comes back to me.

And how I got started talking the legend
    and telling the stories
    and all that stuff—
    I don't know.
Before I knew it I was telling it in different schools
    and going around to different schools,
    and I just got back from a three-weeks tour.
And this lady said,
    "Now tell the story same as you told night before last;
    just try to work it in to what you told."
I said,
    "You're asking me to do something that I'm not used to."
She said,
    "What?"
I said,
    "I'm not teaching school.
    When you're teaching school you've got pen and paper to
        remember the next day where you were."
I said,
    "I can't do that when I'm telling legend stories.
    Every time I go somewhere I have to tell a different story,
    and I don't know how many stories I got in my head.
    Each one never comes out the same story."
And nobody never tells the same stories.
Kathi can't tell my stories.
I can't tell Kathi's stories unless they come out of a book.
It's all in my head, that I tell these different stories.
I tell about the drums that they were playing,
    the elder people that set on the mountains.

➤➤ Elders on the Mountains

I'm going to tell you a little about the Trail of Tears.
Elder man sits on the top of the mountain,
    of each mountain [drumming],
    looking downhill like that
    to see all what all he can see down the valley.
And when he saw it bluish-looking,

that meant there was disease in the air.

The worst disease that they were afraid of back then was diarrhea,
    and now we laugh about the diarrhea
    because we don't have that problem anymore.

We know what kind of medicine to take
    and what kind of medicine to get.

But back then they didn't know.

It caused them to bleed to death,
    and they lost a lot of people to the diarrhea.

So that was the way they would send the message:
    beating, the first drum would pick it up
    and send it on to the next mountain, like that,
    and also when the soldiers were coming to remove the Indian
        people.

And one time this happened during the Trail of Tears.

He saw a man coming way back in the valley,
    and he's looking,
    he's telling:
    "They're on a horse [drumming like hoofbeats],
    they're coming fast, too [faster drumming],
    and they got a gun.
    Get your people together and hide,
    take off up the mountain,
    hide in the cave,
    get away,
    take off as fast as you can."

And the drum would go faster and faster.

"The soldiers are coming faster and faster,
    and they got a gun on their shoulder,
    and they are starting shooting,
    and you can hear it [drumming like gunshots]."

And so that's what happened during the Trail of Tears.

›› The Quail Dance

Back before Columbus' time,
    when the men would hunt the quail,
    we built a fire in the center when the men go out to hunt.

And they bring the food back,
    and then while the water is on, while the food is cooking,
    we dance around the fire to give God thanks,
    and we rejoice what he gave us.
And this is one dance I'm going to do for you, for an example.
While the quail are cooking,
    I'm going to do the quail dance for you.
[Shakes rattle.]
This is the quail dance,
    and you're going to have to help me while I do this
    and holler, say like, when I say, "Whoa-yeh,"
    you say, "Whoo!"
And when I start to dance and when I finish and I say, "Whoa-yeh,"
    then you holler again, "Whoo!"
Whoayeh hey, whoayeh hey
Duyeh hey, Duyeh hey
Whoayeh hey, whoayeh hey
Duyeh hey, Duyeh hey
Whoayeh hey, whoayeh hey
Duyeh hey, Duyeh hey
Whoayeh! Whoo!
[Audience whoops, laughs.]

▶▶ Feathers

Okay, I'm going to tell you a little bit about when I went to
        Oklahoma.
Several years ago
    we went to an amphitheater in Tahlequah, Oklahoma.
When we got off the stage, we got through singing,
    some people met me on the side.
Said,
    "Would you come sing for us in Kansas City?"
I said,
    "Sure, what time do you want us there?
    When do you want us there?"
They said,
    "Tomorrow night 'bout—'round seven o'clock."

I said,
> "Yes, we'll make it."

Said,
> "All right."

So we drove to Kansas City the next night.

And as we drove up,
> people standing around outside the church, looking.

They just kept looking, you know, when we drove up.

And as I got out of the car, and I said,
> "Hi."

And they said,
> "Hi."

And one turned around and said,
> "When are the Indian people coming?" [laughter]

And I said,
> "Well, I'm Indian. I just got here."

I said,
> "Just give us time to set up.
>
> And as soon as we get through setting up,
>
> then we'll sing for you."

They didn't say nothing,
> they just kind of walked around like.

So we got through setting up
> and we went in the church.

So I go in the bathroom and change—
> put on my leather dress and come out.

They said,
> "We want the real Indians." [chuckles from group]

I said,
> "You do?
>
> Well, I'm full-blooded Cherokee Indian,
>
> how much more Indian can I get?" [laughter from group]
>
> "And I'm wearing my costume,
>
> and that's the color that we are, Cherokee Indians."

And one boy said,
> "I want an Indian with the big beautiful feathers on."

I said,
> "Oh, you're not really looking for an Indian,

you're looking for something else.
I said I was full-blooded Cherokee Indian,
I didn't say I was a chicken."
[Group cracks up laughing.]

> ## The Indian Preacher

So I go on from there.
Like I said, I don't know how I got started with the legend stories
            and all that,
    but the more I talk,
    the more I learn.
And this is one story that I learned.
I only tell this to the older people,
    I don't tell this to the children. [laughter]
There was an Indian preacher in a log house.
And back a long time ago, you know,
    in a log house, you could see the cracks through the ceiling,
    you could see even the moon at night.
And they had church,
    and this Indian preacher was there,
    and they were starting,
    and he looked up at the sky and started praying in Indian,
    got down on his knees and closed his eyes
    and prays in Cherokee:
    "Lord, give us the food and the supplies that we really need."
And he opened his mouth,
    and all at once he felt something in his mouth,
    and he went like this [licks lips],
    "Thank you Lord, please give us the food that we need."
And went like this again [licks lips],
    and he looked up and there was a bird sitting there!
[Group cracks up laughing.]

Okay, now I'm going to tell you about something serious.
[Group cracks up even more.]
This is a sad story.

>> The Trail of Tears Basket

There was a basket that was give to me in Oklahoma.
I don't like to talk about the Trail of Tears, but it's really sad.
And sometimes it gets to me, and sometimes I can feel it.
Especially when I got a basket that I carry
　　that's over a hundred and fifty years old,
　　and it's still good and sturdy,
　　and it's a white oak basket that went on the Trail of Tears.
No telling how many people have died in front of this basket.
If this basket could talk to you,
　　there's no telling what all it would tell you
　　that happened along the Trail of Tears:
　　how many people was killed,
　　how many people got hurt
　　and had to be buried beside the road
　　when they couldn't walk.
And no telling what all I could tell
　　from what I listened when I was a little girl.
At the end of the Trail of Tears,
　　when they got to Oklahoma,
　　they had a song that they sung after the hardships
　　and after they had walked far
　　more than a thousand miles
　　and got to Oklahoma.
And this was the song that was sung:
[Edna sings "Oh, How I Love Jesus" in Cherokee.]
Thank you.
[Applause]

Robert Bushyhead

The Reverend Robert Bushyhead was born in 1916 near Cherokee, North Carolina. He grew up in a home where Cherokee was the only language spoken. When he went to a day school, he began to learn English, but it wasn't until he was sent to boarding school in the town of Cherokee, fifteen miles from his home, that he was forced to speak only English. This boarding school was run by the Bureau of Indian Affairs and, like others around the country, attempted to "acculturate" American Indians—into white culture. Bushyhead's experiences at boarding school are like those of many other Cherokee children in the late nineteenth and early twentieth centuries. Because they were punished so severely for using their native language, these Cherokees did not teach their own children to speak it, "lest they be punished as we were."

Throughout his early life, Bushyhead was drawn both to education and to Christianity. Called to the ministry, he traveled all over the United States preaching and speaking. He furthered his education through reading and finally attended Carson-Newman College in Jefferson, Tennessee. When he retired and returned to his home in Cherokee, North Carolina, he acted in the outdoor drama *Unto These Hills*, which tells the story of the Cherokee people and which has been seen by millions of visitors to the Qualla Boundary.

Since the 1960s Reverend Bushyhead has been documenting the Cherokee language, in particular the Kituwah dialect that was originally spoken by the Cherokee people living in the villages along the

Little Tennessee River and its tributaries—the Middle Towns. Several scholars, notably William Cook and Duane King, have worked with Bushyhead to describe the Cherokee language and its grammar, but Bushyhead's most significant work on the language has been taking place since 1991 with the help of his daughter Jean Bushyhead Blanton. Blanton, a schoolteacher, has taken a leave of absence from teaching to help her father with this work. He dictates lessons in the Cherokee language, and these are videotaped. Blanton transcribes the lessons using a word processor. The use of video enables Bushyhead to accurately teach the dialect's inflections and rhythms, which distinguish it from other Cherokee dialects. Bushyhead and Blanton have developed a video dictionary and a computer dictionary that includes guides to oral pronunciation. Sequoyah's original syllabary was developed for a language that people already knew and spoke, and therefore it does not indicate vowel length or accents. Bushyhead has developed a lexical system that adds these to the syllabary but is less complex than the international phonetic system. Bushyhead and Blanton's goal is to produce a series of lessons that can be published as a textbook and used in the Cherokee school system to teach the language at all grade levels, from elementary through high school.

When the Cherokee tribe began running its own school system in 1990, rather than operating under contract to the Bureau of Indian Affairs, it began to encourage the teaching of Cherokee culture and language. In fact, Cherokee culture has played a larger and larger role in the schools, in businesses, and in the public eye. Bushyhead and Blanton's work has been an important part of this process, and in 1996, Reverend Bushyhead was awarded both the Mountain Heritage Award from Western Carolina University and the North Carolina Folk Heritage Award for his contributions to Cherokee culture.

»

The stories in this book were collected during two sessions at Reverend Bushyhead's house. Among them, "The Cherokee Language" describes Robert Bushyhead's early life and his experiences with the Cherokee language, which has always been important to him. "Medicine Stories" is a series of tales including one about collecting medicine plants with his aunt, a healing narrative based on something that happened to him; and a healing narrative about someone else. "The First Time I Saw a White Person— Mrs. Lee" is like a short story, and it is clear that he has told this personal-experience story many times; his translation of "Jesus Loves Me" has been included in the Methodist hymnal. "Yonder Mountain" is a classic folktale with a moral about leadership. "Sequoyah" describes the genius who invented the Cherokee syllabary, a system of eighty-five written symbols that represent all the sounds in the Cherokee language.

"Formula against Screech Owls and Tskilis" describes the use of a medicine formula. A screech owl, in Cherokee traditional belief, may be just a screech owl, or it may be a bad spirit, a "tskili." This formula enables a person to tell the difference. "The Hunter and Thunder" is a rare combination of a myth and a personal-experience story about a medicine formula, explaining the origin of the formula and giving an example of its use in everyday life. The myth part of this narrative is a little like "The Red Man and the Uktena" in Mooney. "The Little People and the Nunnehi" includes several accounts of experiences with these beings whose existence sometimes intersects with the world of the Cherokee. Some stories about them are commonly known folktales like "The Removed Townhouses," while others are personal-experience stories, like these.

The Cherokee Language

As a little boy
    I remember
    the only language spoken in the home
    was Cherokee.
And later I learned other dialects
    and learned also that the one that I was learning at home
    was in the Kituwah dialect,
    and that the Kituwah means "middle" dialect,
    and it was spoken here in this area.
And then later on
    other dialects began to come in,
    and then they got kind of a mixture
    of different dialects.
Now we want to preserve the Kituwah dialect

that our ancestors spoke
    here in the Yellow Hill territory.
I didn't speak English
    until I went to school at Cherokee, North Carolina,
    at the age of seven
    or even later than that.
We had a day school in Bird Town,
    and it had English teachers,
    but yet at home
    we only spoke the Cherokee.
My family talked Cherokee between themselves,
    and yet it was my mother
    who taught me to say things
    and to explain things in the Cherokee language.
Grandma sang a lot.
In the mornings I would waken while she was preparing breakfast,
    and I heard all those old sacred songs
    that she sang in the Cherokee language.
And then later in the years,
    why,
    she let me help her sing,
    and I learned to sing some of those old tunes.
While she was fixing breakfast,
    while she was cooking dinner up,
    she was always singing.
And I spoke only the Cherokee language
    until I started school.
The first school I went to was a day school;
    we went down there,
    and then we went home in the evening.
However, when we moved
    from the Bird Town area
    over into the Whittier area
    on the Thirty-Two-Hundred-Acre Tract
    (this is a distance of fifteen or sixteen or so miles away),
    there were no roads,
    we lived back on the mountain,

and evidently there was no other choice:
    only to put us in a boarding school which they had prepared at
        Cherokee, North Carolina.
This was a government boarding school,
    and when you entered Cherokee,
    one of the first things they taught us was discipline.
And in that line of discipline
    there was a thing that they wouldn't let us do,
    and that was to speak the Cherokee language.
And back at that time,
    our dormitories were heated by steam,
    and they had furnaces under each building,
    and many times we went down into the furnace room,
        where nobody would see us
    and start talking Cherokee.
We would just be getting started good whenever somebody would
        say,
    "All right, boys, let's go to the office."
They had caught us talking Cherokee.
And they punished us as violently for speaking the Cherokee
        language
    as they would have if they caught us smoking or chewing or
        whatever.
So we soon learned that they didn't want us to speak the Cherokee
        language.
And the thing about this was
    that whenever we could not speak the Cherokee language,
    those of us who became parents
    did not teach their children the Cherokee language
    lest they go through that same thing that we had to go through—
        the being punished.
I put out as much effort as I could toward the English language
    because of the fact that my work was going to require
    quite a bit of proper way of speaking the English language.
There was a time that I had spoken,
    and a man came to me, and he said:
    "Since you speak the two languages,

in which language do you think?"
I had never thought about that before,
    and so for a moment I stopped and began to think
    and finally decided that I answer him in this fashion:
    I speak in the language that I'm thinking in.
It's like changing gear—
    you have to stop a moment when you're speaking Cherokee
    and then have to stop your speaking English,
    and you change your thinking in that way.
I have been commended in speaking the English language
    for the fact I speak slowly and distinctly and clearly.
And the Cherokee, when I speak that,
    that's the way Cherokee is set up—
    slow and distinct,
    and it has a flow.
It has a rhythm that is beautiful.
And once you lose that rhythm,
    then, of course, you're lost.
For instance, if I say,
    "Tomorrow I'm going back to my home,"
    there's a rhythm to it.
Someone has explained it in this way:
    it sounds like a waterfall—
    it's that melodious.
One of the most important things is to hear sounds.
And that's why the inflections are so important to me.
"Onion" and "mink" are so different,
    but you spell them the same phonetically,
    and the syllabary symbols are the same,
    but the pronunciation is how you know
        which is which.
There is a thin line there I would mention
    because "onion" has that glottal stop,
    and you know the glottal stop
    is that short period of silence.

I believe for the Cherokee people
    preserving our language is most important.

The language is a possession
    that was given to us by the Great Spirit.
Every effort should be made to retain the most important legacy we
        have,
    which was put in our trust.
I want to get this task accomplished.
As I have said many times before,
    when I think back to my early childhood,
    I remember that it was a place,
    a very, very serene place.
And some of the sounds that I heard
    were from the birds, the animals,
    and other things,
    like the wind blowing through the trees.
And even the storms,
    the thunder and lightning,
    every sound coming from nature.
And it came to the point where that
    my brother and I,
    who was three years older,
    could understand when you heard the birds
    whether it was a mating call,
    whether it was a call of distress.
We could detect those sounds
    and know what was going on.
Of all the heritages that we have,
    I think the language is the most important.
And I may as well go on and say that
    anybody can make a basket,
    anybody can make pottery
    as do the Cherokees as well.
But the language is something that we have
    that no other
    sounds exactly like it.
And we want to preserve this,
    because it is the dialect of the Eastern Band of Cherokees
    in the Yellow Hill territory.

➤➤ Medicine Stories

When I was a little boy
   I believed in Creator,
   the Great Spirit.
And all the created things were,
   you know,
   a part of the creation,
   and they spoke.
Like my Daddy, when he was raising corn,
   in the evening he would say—
   late in the evening he would say,
   "I must go into the field and talk to the corn."
And he—
   what people called—
   had a green thumb.
Everything that he planted
   always came up good
   and yielded much fruit.
And so that was his term:
   "I must go now and talk to my corn."
And then, of course,
   whenever the medication was applied,
   again they would turn to nature.
And the medicine man
   did not go out
   and pick herbs, roots, or barks at random.
He went because he knew
   the Great Spirit would lead him.
And I remember one time
   that a close relative of mine,
   in fact my aunt,
   came to the house.
And the medicine man had sent her out
   to gather some medicine for a sick person.
And she said,
   "Bob, I want you to go with me."

And I went with her.
And on the way to the hillside,
    she explained to me what kind of an herb
    or what kind of a plant
    we were looking for.
And I knew the plant well,
    and when we came to the woods,
    I saw a lot of plants that she had described to me,
    and I knew that was the plant.
And I said,
    "There's one!"
And she came over,
    and she looked at it,
    and she said,
    "No, that's not the one."
Yet I knew and realized
    that that was the plant she had described.
So I didn't say anything,
    just kept on going with her,
    knowing that she had something else
    that I should learn.
And maybe it was because she wanted me to learn
    is the reason she took me along with her—
    I realized that later.
And whenever we were along the hillside,
    I saw many, many plants like the one she had described to me,
    and each time she would say,
    "No, that's not the one."
And then after a while,
    she said,
    "Bob, come up here.
    There's the plant."
And it was the same species of plant that I had been showing to her,
    and she had said, "That isn't it."
So I went on up there,
    and I saw the plant,
    the same kind I had been pointing out.

But this time
   this particular plant
   was shaking in the wind.
And in the breeze—let me use the word breeze—
   in the breeze,
   and there was no breeze,
   that plant was trembling.
And she said,
   "That's it, that's the one."
And so by that
   you know she had some kind of spiritual guidance
   as to find which plant she was looking for.
And then
   she carefully dug the root out of that ground.
And the plant—
   when she broke the root from the plant,
   she shoved that plant back into the ground
   after she had removed the root.
And then she said,
   "We have to be sure,
   we have to be sure,
   because the sick person is depending on us,
   the medicine man is depending on us to get the right herb."
And so she said,
   "Let's take it down to the creek."
And we took off from the hillside
   down to the creek,
   and she took that root and washed the dirt off of it.
And then she put that root in the palm of her hand
   and stood there
   just for a minute or so.
And without any encouragement,
   the root turned over in her hand.
And she said,
   "That's it. That's it."
And then she took that root back to the medicine man,
   and the medicine man worked with that root

and prepared that root,
and the patient got well.

So I guess maybe it was a lesson that she wanted me to learn:
that you just don't go out into the woods and pick herbs at
random.
And one for each one,
and that's where the clan comes in.
You name the person,
but as you're naming the person,
you have to know what clan they are:
the wolf clan, the deer clan, or the paint clan,
or whatever clan that they might be,
and there are seven.
And you have to know the clan of the patient you are treating,
because you're asking for this medicine from the Great Spirit,
and he directs all of your movements.
And that plant was for that particular man and particular clan.
And so I think that
during this time
the Indian looked to nature for guidance
in all the activities of his undertakings.
I think that I can verify
just the thing that we have been talking about
as being true,
because it happened to me at one time.
And I had been sick five months,
I mean bedfast.
I had gone to the hospital,
the government hospital in Cherokee,
and they had tried everything in the book,
but I still could not recover.
And one day my daddy was at the house,
and he was pulling down some logs with a steer for firewood,
and I began to think about:
when a medicine man is trained and treated to become a
medicine man,

he doesn't volunteer to anybody
    to do anything for them.
He has to be asked by the individual himself
    before he can do any good.
And so I began to think:
    he may know something, but he won't say:
    "I know this, I know that,
    and I want to help you, I want to heal you."
He didn't say that.
And when he came to the house, I asked him,
    "Do you know of any way that I can be treated for this ailment?"
And he said,
    "Yes, there are ways."
And I said,
    "Would you be willing to help me and get me healed from this
        disease?"
And he didn't say,
    "I will," or "I will do it."
He said,
    "I'll try."
And he gave a treatment,
    and he would whisper the words from his lips,
    the formula that they used,
    and then he would blow me in the face seven times.
And then—that's all he did.
And no medication of any kind.
As he repeated this formula,
    I could notice by looking at him
    that he was speaking to someone or something.
And after that treatment that night,
    the wife was sitting by my bed at night
    and watching over me.
And she saw a tiny ball of fire
    come out from under my pillow.
And back in those days,
    we didn't have ceilings, just a thick loft.
And she noticed that ball of fire
    came out from under my pillow

and circled upward,
    and when it came to the loft,
        that loft didn't even stop him,
    it just went on through the loft and out.
And from that day forth,
    I began to recover.
And after seven days I was able to go back to work.
And you see,
    there's quite a bit of difference
    in seven days
    and three or four months of suffering.
So that made me feel also that
    the Great Spirit,
    the Creator of all the world,
    had things fixed so that one could serve the other.
And I think that I have seen,
    many, many, many times,
    people being healed.
The medicine man didn't take the initiative,
    and that's why a lot of it is lost,
    because they didn't take the initiative.
They didn't say,
    "You have to learn this,"
    or "You should learn this,"
    or "You should read this,"
    see, you had to ask.
Like, for instance, another case.
Now I didn't see this, I just heard about this.
A man was traveling,
    and he slept in another man's house.
And this man was sitting there
    with his foot up on a banister of the porch,
    and his leg was swollen, just ready to burst,
    and it was already seeping with liquid.
And he came by,
    and he said,
    "Look at your leg—you must like it that way."
That was an invitation—"You must like it that way."

What he was actually trying to say was,
    "Why don't you get somebody to help you?"
He said,
    "No, I don't like it that way,
    and if there's anything that you can do,
    I would like you to help us,"
    and he said,
    "Of course I want you to help me.
    I want you to help me."
And the medicine man said,
    "I'll try. I'll try."
And there was some boys playing around in the yard,
    and he told those boys,
    he said,
    "As I came into the trail leading to this house,
    I noticed down the trail there's a dead oak tree,
        dead, still standing,
    and the bark that fell from it is still lying around the foot of that
            oak tree.
    Would you bring me some of that?"
So the boys ran down there
    and brought an armload of dry bark apiece.
And he took this bark,
    when the boys presented it to him,
    to the fireplace.
And he lighted the fire
    and started the fire with that bark
    until there was nothing left
    except a heap of coals.
And then when he got ready,
    then he told the man, he said,
    "All right, I'm going to doctor you now."
And he came back into the house
    and sat the man in front of the fireplace,
    and he took his hands
    and held them close over that pile of coals
    until his hands were hot.
Then he came back

and started at the bottom, just above his ankle,
and came up
and cupped his hands as though he had something in his hands,
   carried them over to the fireplace and turned his hands over,
and you could hear a sputtering
   as though something was going into the fire.
And seven times he did that.
The seventh time
   that he went back to the fireplace
   and opened his hands over the fire,
   there was nothing.
No sputterings,
   nothing.
And he said,
   "Okay."
He said,
   "I guess we've got you,
   we've got it now."
The seventh time he did that,
   just like that there was no swelling.
And so fire also was a very, very sacred item
   in the work of the medicine man,
   and the fire was never allowed to go out
   in the home at any time.
He said, "That's all."
He said, "I'll come back in a day or two
   to see whether you're dead or not." [laughs]
And then another thing is
   that they don't charge you a fee for treatments.
They can't,
   they're not allowed to,
   but in order to repay them
   you volunteer to give them what they need,
   what you want them to have.
A couple of days later the man came back,
   and all that was dried up, was healing,
   and the man said,
   "Well, what do I owe you for helping me?"

"Oh," he said,
    "If you talk bad about me sometime in the future
    that will be pay enough for me."
He meant, "You can come to my defense,
    I'm not as bad as they say I am."
You know, if somebody says something bad about me,
    you know better,
    can tell him differently.
He meant, "I've done something good for you,
    now if somebody says something bad about me
    you can say something good about me in my behalf."
And usually that's a good way to stop criticism,
    if anybody wants to say something bad about you
    and I say,
    "Well you know, I kind of like her, this is what I like about her,"
    then that kind of stops that.
I would think that would be the same meaning.
One of the accomplishments among the Cherokees
    is that if they disagree, they don't argue.
Change the subject.
And that's a good way to stop an argument,
    'cause it takes two to argue.

➤➤ The First Time I Saw a White Person—Mrs. Lee

When I was about—
    oh, I'd say-
    between five and six years old,
    I had heard stories.
Because back in those days,
    they invited storytellers
    to come into the home,
    and such was true in my home.
My daddy and my mama would ask individuals to come into our
            home
    and tell us stories
    about their ancestors

and about their past.
And the one thing I remembered—
    and this was so true
    as I was working in the drama for seventeen years—
    that there was a time when the Cherokees were removed
        from the East to the West.
And they were driven along the Trail of Tears
    for three long winter months.
And one-third of the Cherokee died
    on the Trail of Tears.
And I could just see the small children taken sick
    and dying along the trail.
I could see those who were already sick when they started
    dying on the Trail of Tears.
And I could see the older people,
    the old and aged and helpless people
    being driven at gunpoint from day to day,
    dying on the Trail of Tears.
And so after hearing these stories,
    this one particular story stuck in my mind,
    not knowing that I would be taking part in the drama
        showing this dreadful dark space of history
        concerning the Cherokee Indian.
But anyway,
    there was a little hate,
    a little hate created in my heart
    for the white man.
Even though I had never seen a white man,
    I hated him.
I hated him.
And so one day
    my mother came to us and said,
    "There's somebody coming up the trail."
And we had a little makeshift window
    where we had pushed the punching out of the—
    from between the logs—
    and a makeshift window
    where we could look down the trail.

And sure enough
    we ran to that place
    and looked down the trail,
    and there was somebody coming up the trail.
There were two people coming up the trail,
    and they were not Indians,
    they were not Indians.
The first thing I felt was fear.
Fear.
Knowing what had happened to the Cherokees
    when they were driven west,
    I made for the darkest corner,
    and my brother,
    who was just three years older,
    sat down in front of me,
    so as to protect me
    from anything that might happen.
They came to the house,
    and the man stopped and talked to my daddy,
    and the lady came into the house.
And they were the Reverend J. M. Lee and his wife,
    had come as missionaries to the Cherokees.
And as they talked on the outside,
    and my brother was sitting in front of me,
    Mrs. Lee came into the house.
She was old,
    she was white-headed,
    she was wrinkled,
    and she had glasses on.
And to me,
    as a small boy,
    that was the most *ferocious* thing I had ever seen in my life.
But anyway, she came on in,
    made her way to the corner where we were sitting,
    and she began to talk to us.
We didn't understand what she was saying—
    we *couldn't* understand what she was saying—
    but the tone of her voice,

the tone of her voice
    told us she loved us.
She loved us.
She loved us.
And then she would say something like,
    "Jesus, Jesus loves you.
    Even though your clothes are tattered and torn,
    and your face is soiled from playing outside,
    Jesus loves you."
And then she said,
    "I love you,
    I love you."
The tone of her voice told us volumes.
And so
    that little hate that I had created in my heart
    began to melt,
    began to melt.
Because I had thought that the white man,
    when they said
    the white man drove the Cherokee from their homes,
    I thought of the white man much like I would think of a
           snowman—
    white from top to bottom.
But I learned that they were also people.
After several days of this—
    because they made their way to our home,
    they didn't have a home to live in,
    and wherever night caught them,
    that's where they stayed all night.
And so they went from home to home,
    but each morning they'd come by our home about the same
           time,
    and many times found us waiting in that makeshift window,
    looking down the trail,
    waiting for her to come.
And she would come on up and tell us that,
    "Jesus loves you,
    Jesus loves you."

And then,
    "I love you.
    I love you.
    And Jesus wants you to love him.
    Jesus wants you to love him.
    And Jesus wants you to love me."
And so on,
    just stories,
    little items like that from day to day.
And, I guess, one day
    she figured it was time for us to graduate from that class,
    so she led us away from the house,
        across a big stream,
    and she found some yellow flint stones
    and placed them under the tree.
And there she told us to sit down.
Then she would tell us the story of Jesus.
Back in those days,
    the aprons that women wore
    had pockets on the inside.
She would reach inside her pockets and show us a picture.
Then she would say,
    "Jesus. Jesus. Jesus.
    Jesus loves you.
    Jesus wants you to love him.
    Jesus wants you to love me.
    Jesus wants us to love each other."
Things like that,
    just little bits of information she was giving to us.
So one day
    she led us across the creek,
    placed us on those yellow stones,
    and reached into her inside apron pocket
    and pulled out a picture of Jesus.
And I had heard that name so many times,
    when I saw that picture,
    I beat her to the draw,
    I said,

"Jesus, Jesus."
And she said,
    "Yes, yes, Jesus."
And she hand'ed the card to me
    and she said,
    "You may have this. This is yours. This is yours."
And when my brother noticed
    that I received a card for saying Jesus,
    he said,
    "Jesus, Jesus."
And many times
    I think about
    that that was the first word,
    outside of the Cherokee language,
    that I had spoken.
This time,
    in English, I had said,
    "Jesus."
And seemed like it gave me some kind of satisfaction
    to know that as I learned other languages,
    "Jesus" was the first word that I learned.
And then, from then on,
    day after day,
    she would take a different picture.
And after each session,
    she would give us that card.
We saw Jesus as he fed the multitudes.
We saw Jesus as he raised the dead.
We saw Jesus as he healed the sick.
We saw Jesus even when he hung on the cross
    because he loved us.
I was very superstitious in those days,
    and at night I would awaken and say,
    "Joel, I'm scared, I'm scared."
He'd say,
    "What are you afraid of?"
I says,
    "I don't know, I don't know."

And as a habit,
    my daddy would just pile up the coals
    and cover them with ashes at night
    so the fire wouldn't go out.
And then I would say,
    "Let's look at Jesus again."
And together we would get up from bed
    and get our pictures from under the pillow
    and carry them to the hearth,
    and we scattered the coals out a little bit to have a light.
And there on the hearth
    we would look at Jesus again,
    looking through all our cards.
And then we went back to sleep,
    put the pictures under the pillow again,
    and I could go to sleep,
    knowing that Jesus was under the pillow.
And then,
    of course, I had to go to boarding school,
    and for a long time I didn't see Mrs. Lee anymore.
But there in school,
    we had a two-story dormitory with banisters going,
    leading up the stairs.
And one day
    I heard somebody yell from the downstairs hall saying,
    "Robert, there's somebody here to see you."
And I thought,
    "My mother!
    My mother has come to see me."
I ran down the hall,
    turned backward on the banister,
    slid to the first floor,
    and walked down the hall,
    but I was still saying,
    "My mother, my—"
No, it wasn't my mother,
    it was Mrs. Lee,
    Mrs. Lee.

And she said,
    "I just had to see you again."
And she said,
    "We have our mission church built now.
    And we have church, we have services,
    we talk about Jesus there in that church."
And she said, "I want you to come. I want you to attend our church."
And from the window I could see the church,
    it was just that close, you know, down the road from the school.
And then I thought about the fact
    that we could not leave the school campus.
We had a wall all around the campus
    and had little gates where people went in and out.
And they had a guard at every gate
    so no student could go on the outside.
Then I said,
    "I can't, I can't."
She said, "Why?"
She said—I told her,
    "I can't get out of the gate.
    I can't get out through the gate.
    There's guards there."
And she said,
    "Don't worry. Don't worry."
She patted me on the back and said,
    "Don't worry.
    All of that has been taken care of.
    Just show them this card."
And, you know, she gave me a card,
    and next Sunday I had gotten ready to go to the church,
    I went to the matron—she fixed me up real neat, you know,
    to go to church.
And when I came to the gate,
    I held up that card,
    and they said,
    "Okay, go on out."
And she had told me
    that when you come to the building,

come on up to the balcony.
I had no idea what the balcony was.
And so when I came,
    my first question after arriving at the mission was
    asking a gentleman standing at the door,
    "Where is the balcony?"
And he pointed to the rear of the church, up to the balcony.
And there when I looked,
    there was Mrs. Lee standing up there waiting,
    and she was just gesturing to me to come on up.
And I went on up the stairs, into the balcony,
    and there were several children there in her class,
    and she introduced me to all of them,
    and she told them about how—that she had been in my home.
And there I learned more and more about Jesus.
The thing that struck me most
    was that now I could understand what she was saying.
I could understand,
    after being in school a while,
    I could understand English enough to know what she was saying
        to us.
And she again taught us about Jesus, Jesus, Jesus.
And all the stories of his feeding the five thousand,
    the stories about how that he healed the sick,
    stories about how that he died on the cross for us.
Yes, Jesus loved us.
And I suppose that was the first song I ever learned,
    "Jesus loves me, this I know
    For the Bible tells me so."
And in Cherokee it is:

    Jee-suh gee gey yoo hee
    Go wehl ah kee no hee seh
    Joo nah stee kah joo jeh lee
    Oo hlee nee kee dee yeh no.

    Jee-suh gee gey yoo
    Jee-suh gee gey yoo

Jee-suh gee gey yoo
Ah gee no hee seh no.

and so on down the line.
But that's what we learned.
And then
before our class was ended,
she handed each of us a penny,
a penny.
And then
at the head of the stairs where the post was,
she would place a basket.
And after the class was over,
and we were dismissed,
why, she'd place that basket there,
and we would take these pennies that she had put into our hands
and drop them into the basket as we left the balcony.
She was teaching us to give.
And I will never forget
even that little song that we sang
as we put our pennies into the basket,
marching out.
And that little song that she taught us all was,
"Dropping, dropping, dropping, dropping,
we will take them all.
Every one to Jesus, we will take them all."
She was teaching us to give to Jesus who loved us,
and whom we loved,
and who had done so many things for us
that we loved him.
This was a starting point.
And one day we went up there,
after several months of this,
we went up there,
and there was another lady there.
Mrs. Lee was not there.
And she told us,
as the class met, she said,

"There's something I need to tell you,
there's something that I need to tell you.
The Lord told Mrs. Lee,
    'This is enough. You can come home now.'
She won't be here anymore,
but she will be waiting when we get to Heaven,
she'll be there."
And she was buried in Dalton, Georgia.
On a little hill in Dalton, Georgia,
    there's a little grave that says, "Here . . ."
The headstone says,
    "Here lies Mrs. Lee,
    pioneer missionary to the Cherokee Indians."
And then a little string of flowers,
    and underneath that string of flowers are the words:
    "She was faithful unto death."
And that was the beginning.
At the age of sixteen, I was saved.
I joined the church and was baptized.
And I was baptized by my grandfather in the Tuckaseegee River,
    and from then on,
    why just one thing led to the other.
But I will never forget the basic teaching of Mrs. Lee
    that Jesus loves me.

➤➤ Yonder Mountain

This is a story that I really like because,
    not only because of its beauty,
    but because of its teaching,
    the teaching.
The story goes
    that there was an old chief.
This chief,
    even though he was now so old,
    he could not lead his people to wars
    as he had in many, many days
    where he led them to victory over the enemy.

Now he was old,
   so he called three of his favorite men to him.
And he told them, he said,
    "One of you is going to become chief.
    One of you is going to take my place.
    But I'll have to put you to the test.
And he said,
    "Do you see yonder mountain?"
And they looked way out in the beyond;
   they saw a mountain.
And he told them, he said,
    "I want you to go to that mountaintop.
    Bring me back what you find there."
So they leaped with joy
   and in a running fashion left the chief
   to do his bidding.
The first one we shall mention
   is the one who started up the mountain toward the
        mountaintop.
And he came to a place
   where there were precious stones on each side of the trail.
And he said,
    "If we had these as trade items, we would never hunger
       anymore,
    we'd just use them as trade items, and life would be much
       better."
So he gathered some of these stones and went back.
And whenever the community saw him coming,
   a great shout of joy went up
   as he came into the gate
   and came unto the chief and said,
    "Chief, look what I found—precious stones.
   We need no longer go hungry.
   We use these as trade items and have anything we want."
And the chief smiled fondly upon him and said,
    "You have done well. You have done well.
   But let's wait for the other man."
The other man went on up farther than the precious stones

until he came to a place where—
   that he looked on each side of the trail
   and there saw all types of herbs, roots, barks, leaves,
   the healing elements of a medicine man.
And he said,
   "If we had these, we would no longer have to suffer.
   We could heal ourselves with these herbs."
He went back down,
   and the same cheer went up as they saw him coming in
   and went to the gate,
   the chief went to the gate to meet him.
And he said,
   "Chief, look what I have found—herbs of all descriptions.
   We no longer need to suffer, we can heal ourselves now."
And the chief again smiled upon him fondly and said,
   "You have done well,
   but let's wait on the third man."
They waited.
Days went by.
He didn't return.
They waited.
And the people said,
   "Something must have happened to him.
   Why wait any longer?"
And the chief said,
   "Let's wait one more day."
They waited,
   and the next day
   they saw the third man
   coming up the trail.
He was staggering,
   he was unsteady with his steps
   as he came to the gate.
And he told the chief, he said,
   "I went to yonder mountain.
   I have nothing in my hands that I have brought from the
         mountaintop.

I passed a place where there were precious stones.
I passed a place where there were precious stones, but I
       remembered
that you said to the top of yonder mountain.
So I went on.
Finally I came to a place
where there were herbs of all descriptions on every side.
But there again, I remembered
that you said to the top of yonder mountain."
And he said,
    "I went to the top, chief.
    The road is rough, with many thorns
    and with many rocks to hurt your feet and to cut your feet."
And he pointed to his bloody feet, his torn clothes.
And he said,
    "Chief, I went to yonder mountain.
    I don't bring anything in my hand,
    but I have a story to tell you.
    As I stood on yonder mountain and looked far beyond the
       mountain,
    I saw a smoke signal.
    And there was an SOS.
    There are people over there, they're dying.
    But as I read the smoke signals,
    they want somebody to come and help them."
And he said,
    "Chief, we need somebody to go over there.
    We need to go over there and help them,
    for they are dying."
Already the chief was wrapping the chief's cloak around him,
    and said,
    "You shall be our next chief.
    We need a man who has been to the top of the mountain
    and saw beyond the mountain
    other people who are in need.
    Yes, you will be our next chief."

›› Sequoyah

Sequoyah?
I admire that man.
Sequoyah was a very, very successful businessman,
    and he did a lot for his people, and even fought in the wars with
        them.
In the eyes of the people he is a genius.
Nobody has accomplished anything like he developed.
He was an important man.
And like, for instance:
    he decided one day
    that if white man could put talk on paper,
    so can the Cherokee.
And how this came about was:
    one day
    he was sitting by the creek,
    on the banks of the creek,
    and the wind blew a newspaper before him.
He took it.
He couldn't read it.
And now that's where he said:
    "If white man can put talk on paper,
    so can the Cherokee."
And then he began.
Now here's the genius part.
Just by hearing people talk,
    he captured those sounds
    and gave them syllables.
How many sounds are there?
He set himself to the task,
    and he captured those sounds.
And he resigned from all of his responsible positions
    and hid himself away from the crowds
    and sat in dark corners
    uttering strange sounds.
This gave a mistaken idea
    that something mentally had happened to Sequoyah.

And so they began to hear
    that maybe he was mentally ill.
His wife,
    even as she sat in the home,
    and he sitting in the dark corner of the home
    uttering strange sounds,
    had the idea that perhaps he was going mentally ill.
And she ousted him.
He went out of the house,
    and he built a little cabin down next to the river,
    and there he worked for two years.
And as he lingered among the people,
    he learned
    as they talked
    to capture sounds.
And that is amazing!
To capture sounds just by hearing somebody talk
    and recording them in the crude way that he had:
        some on bark,
        some on carvings,
        some on paper with pokeberry juice for ink,
        and so on down the line.
He learned the sounds of the Cherokee language,
    and to me that is the most wonderful thing
    that has ever happened.
And then whenever he worked
    two years in that cabin,
    his wife went down
    and burned down the cabin.
Two years work
    roared into flames.
Then even his neighbors
    there in that town,
    even they ousted him,
    and so he left.
And when he left, his daughter went with him.
But he didn't cease
    studying and compiling

the alphabet which he was busy making.
And after he had completed this,
   which was a period of about twelve years,
   his daughter traveling with him,
   went to Texas, went to Mexico,
   round and about,
   and finally, after twelve years,
   completed what he called the Cherokee alphabet.
When he came back to his people,
   they were still a little leery,
   and they were still not willing to accept what he said
   when he told them that,
   "I have completed the Cherokee language.
   And I have completed the syllabary.
   I have captured the sounds,
   And I have put them into print."
Now the print that he had
   was a borrowed print
   taken from the English speller and the Greek testament,
   and he borrowed sounds from them.
For he found that
   with all of the sounds that he had captured
   and was wanting to make syllables out of them,
   that he found it very, very difficult.
And after twelve years he just resigned himself to the fact
   he could borrow these from an English speller and a Greek
      testament.
And so you will find a capital "Y" and a capital "W"
   and you will find a capital "T"
   and so on in the alphabet,
   but they have their own sounds.
And when he came back to his people
   and told of his accomplishments,
   they were still leery
   and would not believe him,
   would not accept him.
And he told them,
   "I'll tell you what we'll do.

My daughter has been with me these twelve years.
And if you will send her out of the room
and then you tell me what you want me to write,
why, I will do that.
And then we'll call her back in
and let her read to you
what you told me to write."
So they did that,
after they had told him what they wanted him to write,
why, they called the daughter back in.
And when she read it
back to the Cherokee council,
it was exactly as they told him how to read.
And she read it,
and it was word for word
what they had told him to write.
And then they accepted that.
There are eighty-five characters,
and each one had a sound.
Now he did not use any inflections at all,
because he was writing for a people
that already knew how to say the words.
To a nonspeaker,
we would have to put those inflections in
so they can be pronounced properly,
correctly,
and so they could be understood.
Because the inflections are those markings that give the sounds
differently
and can change the sound of the word
as well as the meaning of the word.
So we have to teach it that way to nonspeakers
so they can say it properly.
Now then,
whenever he was accepted,
the Cherokee became very interested.
And in a very short while—
now imagine that—

in a very short while,
they were reading
and they were writing
the Cherokee language.
So he had accomplished his purpose,
even though he suffered quite a bit of setbacks
along the way.
And that's all we have now.
Now, the different sections:
now this is the Kituwah, as I said before,
because it is Yellow Hill territory.
The people in Graham County were living in Overhill territory, see,
a different dialect.
Dialects change due to location, even English does, actually.
You don't have to go any further than Virginia,
if you hear the word "house" pronounced "hoos."

>> Formula against Screech Owls and Tskílís

Well, now I'll have to start a little further back.
My daddy said that the Cherokee had a way of becoming able to
practice witchcraft.
Now today we look at witchcraft
as something evil,
but it's not.
He said that a person was treated at a very early age
by the medicine man
to become a good hunter or whatever,
and also the ability to change himself into another figure
spiritually.
For instance,
if they were deerhunting,
why, he could change himself into the form of a deer
spiritually,
but he would be here.
And he could go out there among the deer
and tell which way they were traveling
and how fast they were traveling.

And then he would come and report to the hunters;
    they would go ahead the way they were traveling
    and were there waiting when the deer arrived.
Good things like that, see.
And like everything else,
    I guess,
    the human race
    if he has a good thing, he can make evil out of it.
And so that's what happens, see.
I was—
    just for one example—
    I was very superstitious when I heard the screech owl:
    that was *somebody*, and he was there to do us harm.
And I was very superstitious when I heard it screech.
And my mother cured that
    when she said,
    "Now, there's a way to find out whether it's a real owl,
    or whether it's a witch."
And she taught me that,
    and Jean [his daughter], I think we worked on that, too.
And it has worked,
    it has worked.
If it's an owl,
    it gets fainter and fainter and away.
And I was out once
    with a group of Scouts;
    they had a meeting out,
    had a big campfire,
    and a screech owl happened to come,
    and he begin to make noise just around there.
And I turned around and I said the formula.
Now the leader of this group said,
    "What did you do?"
Said,
    "I noticed that you turned around when you heard that screech
        owl."
I told him what my mother had told me,
    and he said,

"Would you teach me that?"
I said,
    "Yes, I'll do better than that,
    I'll put it on tape so you hear it and learn to say it."
About two years later
    he came back in the area without the boys,
    just as a visit,
    and he said,
    "It works, it works. After two years, it works."
I said,
    "What works?"
He said,
    "That formula to chase the owl away."
He said,
    "I tried it and it works."
It works for anybody who knows that formula.
In English, you're saying:
    "A lot of non-Indians,"
    or, if you want to put it this way,
    "There are a lot of those without a clan,
    and they are coming,
    and they are going to catch you,
    they are going to kill you,
    they are going to cut your head off with a lot of swords.
    Here come those who are without a clan,
    who are non-Indians,
    and they are carrying their swords with them,
    they're going to cut your head off,
    they're going to kill you,
    run away."
And he runs away.
You just say it to yourself,
    and that's just one of the many, many, many formulas.

›› **The Hunter and Thunder**

[Jean:]
Most of these formulas that you're talking about have been lost.
We do not know what many of the formulas are anymore.
I know that there's a story, Daddy—
    well, not a story,
    it actually happened—
    where my grandmother said a formula.
They always said you could see their lips moving but couldn't hear
        them.
Can you tell that experience about how
    she used to send the storms away
    if it was going to—
    if she was afraid it was going to destroy their crops?
[Robert:]
Well, that's the idea,
    it was for protection.
Now we would have to go back
    to the thunder and the man and the serpent.
A hunter,
    as I stated before,
    was treated by the medicine man while he was still a baby
    to be successful.
And then to know,
    to understand the ways of nature so far as animals are concerned.
And this man was such.
And he went out several times,
    many, many times,
    to feed the family,
    to feed the whole village sometimes.
And so he was very successful.
Hardly ever did he come home without anything.
But this day,
    he went out,
    he had no success.
No success at all in any form.
And around about noon

he sat down
   under a tree
   and was sitting there
   when he heard a call:
   "Help me, help me, help me."
And as a hunter
   he had keen ears;
   he was trying to get the direction
   from which the sound came.
And he paused,
   and when he reached the top of the hill,
   he looked down in the valley.
And there in the valley was a hunter,
   and this hunter was saying,
   "Help me, help me, help me."
And the snake was coiled around him, and
   squeezing, squeezing, squeezing,
   until that man's voice was very weak.
And when the hunter approached him,
   he said,
   "Help, help, help."
And the serpent said,
   "No, help me, help me,
   let's kill this man."
And the man said,
   very faintly,
   "Do you want to help me?
   Shoot this snake on the seventh spot on his neck."
Well, you know,
   he didn't have very much choice,
   he chose to help the man.
And he put his arrow into his bow,
   and with a twang the arrow left the bow
   and went straight to his mark
   into the seventh spot on the serpent.
And he began to uncoil,
   and he fell dead.
   [Slaps hand for sound of falling.]

Then he went and helped this man up
  and stayed with him,
  and he said,
  after he stood there a few minutes and got his strength back,
  said to this hunter,
  "Let's go over to the top of the hill,
  I'll have something to tell you."
They went on up the hill and sat down,
  and the man said,
  "My name is Thunder,
  and you can refer to me as Uncle,
  and you did me a great favor today.
  Now, I like to destroy things,
  I like, you know, to have fun.
  But if there's anything that would hurt you,
  all you have to do is talk to me."
And he gave him this formula,
  gave him the formula, see.
And that, like Jean just said,
  that formula is probably lost.
We have made researches here,
  researches there,
  researches among old people.
We have one more possibility,
  that that man may know that formula.
And he's a very old man.
I think some of the reasons that so many have been lost—
  we put off seeing these old people
  who have passed away.
Many times my regrets are:
  why didn't I ask my daddy this?
He's gone now, see.
Well, anyway, my mother knew this formula,
  therefore I felt,
  why didn't I learn it?
Now she's dead,
  no point.
And so, like she said before,

like Jean said before,
I could tell when there were—
you've seen storms rising,
black clouds mixed with white clouds,
you know, coming in the direction.
When that would happen,
she would say,
"Boys, be quiet,
sit over there in the corner."
And then she would stand at the edge of the porch,
and like Jean said,
I could tell she was saying something.
And this storm was coming,
and she was worried about her crops;
they were near the harvest stage.
And then she would stand on the porch
and say this formula.
Then she would go blow right into the middle of an oncoming
storm,
blow this way,
blow this way,
and then she would say the formula again,
but this time she would blow this way,
she would blow this way.
And after a while
we would see,
after seven times,
she said it seven times,
and then after the seventh time,
we would see a little clear spot
formed in that part of the storm
where she blew this way,
in that part of the storm
she blew this way.
Now if somebody just told me that,
I wouldn't know whether to believe it or not.
But I saw it.
See, I saw it.

I know what it was.
So the storm would miss us.
The storm would move around
    the crops that she was trying to protect.
Many, many are the things that we have seen.

► The Little People and the Nunnehi

Now the Little People.
This really happened
    through the aid of the medicine man,
    and some of the leaders of the tribe
    would get together,
    and they would learn these things.
And if anyone wanted to employ the Little People—
    in Cherokee "Nunnehi"—
    they're not born, they don't die, Nunnehi.
They're like spirits,
    and they could implore them to come,
    and there are some who have seen them.
Now you can't see them
    unless they want you to see them.
And if you see them,
    there's something going to happen
    whether good or bad,
    either way.
Now we have some younger people,
    that Dakota, she saw them
    when her mother died.
Now when her mother Maggie died—
    those who employed them,
    they talked to them before they died, that:
    "If I should die you go back to your home,"
    and they do.
And in this case,
    the mother must have employed some,
    and her daughter says
    when she died,

they saw this little man walk out
    and down the hall, and left.
And my mother even told me this,
    about the Nunnehi.
And "immortals" is what I'm saying now,
    they're immortals.
And she said that her mother told her one day,
    said,
        "Let's go over and see our neighbor,"
        who was an older woman, and
        "Let's go see her, she's bad off,"
        see.
And whenever they arrived,
    she told my mother, said,
        "Sit here on the porch."
They had a high porch, see.
She sat on the porch with her feet hanging down.
She said,
        "That woman's not going to last long,"
    and went back in.
And she was sitting out there.
And it wasn't a very,
    but a few moments
    when she heard people screaming and crying,
    and she knew that the lady had died.
And as she set there,
    of course the lights from the lamp shone out into the yard,
    and she saw a little man
    walk out from under the front porch
    and go on out,
    went halfway across the yard
    and turned around,
    and went back at the house,
    and turned and vanished into the yard.
She had talked to that immortal,
    and he left.
Now there are those who have some of this,
    but don't have time to tell of it all to me,

and they died.
There's a place in Whittier where my uncle lives.
Now I know he had them,
    because there were too many evidences to say otherwise.
For instance,
    he and I went to visit his sister across the hill,
    and we sat there and talked with them
    till around about midnight,
    and then we went up the hill,
        up the edge of the hill,
        to the ridge,
    and followed the ridge, and then on down to his house.
And we were sitting at the edge of the fields,
    and he said,
    "Let's sit down here a while and talk."
And we had not been sitting there very long,
    until we'd seen a wall of fire
    come up across from the other side of the mountain,
    and it traveled at treetop height
    all the way down to the creek.
And it turned and went down toward his sister's house,
    and then went to the spring,
    and it rose back up again
    and followed the same track back over the mountain.
And he said,
    "Hmm, what does that mean?"
And about that time,
    you know how you can take a rock
    and make it fling, "ktum,"
    we heard that sound,
    and it hit a tree right next to us.
And he just laughed.
He said,
    "I guess we'll just have to go."
He said they always do that,
    meaning the Little People,
    I guess they go look for him
    whenever he's away.

And we went back home—
    and the trail led around to the back of his cabin—
    so he had to go to the back and walk around to the front.
And just when we stepped off to the corner of the house
    we heard that same sound,
    and it [makes smacking sound with hands]
    hit a tree right next to us.
And he just laughed.
He said,
    "They are coming with us, but don't worry about it."
And then we talked a few minutes,
    and I told him I guess I better go,
    I guess the time was to go.
And I lived about two houses away from there.
He told me, days later,
    he said,
    "Did you see anybody when you left here the other night?"
I said,
    "No, in fact I ran from the house all the way home,
    and I didn't see anybody."
And he said there was someone who was walking slowly,
    and someone was haunting him—
    so that remains—
    whatever.
And so I think that they are real,
    they are there.
And like I said,
    if you don't have time to talk to them,
    they'll see that,
    and nobody had better not go there
    because they would raise a fuss.
For instance,
    my oldest boy
    and my next-to-the-oldest boy
    went to this place,
    I guess more or less to experiment.
And they knew that he had had them,
    and they had heard everything when they were growing up.

Well, this time,
  before they arrived to the location
  they heard somebody,
  like dipping water out of a spring into a bucket,
  they could hear that noise.
But they went on and on,
  and just before they arrived,
  before the house had been located,
  they heard these same sounds,
  drops in a bucket.
And oh, they ran from that place.
And my oldest boy said,
  "I thought I could run fast,
  but Richard passed me." [laughs]
And just incidences like that.
And Lucy Armortain in the Big Cove area said she saw one.
And this one did not have any clothes on,
  the others I mentioned had clothes on.
This one did not have a stitch of clothing on him
  and was lying on a limb that went over a river.
And he was lying there,
  but she could never explain why
  or, you know.
So there are evidences,
  and you can hear them make noises,
  you can hear them, you know,
  in different ways, walking and, you know.
They are not mischievous.
They are protectors.

Marie Junaluska

Marie L. Junaluska is one of the few members of the younger generation who grew up speaking Cherokee. Recognized as an outstanding translator, she has worked on a project for the Eastern Band—translating original articles from the *Cherokee Phoenix* newspaper from Cherokee into English—and has worked as a language and culture teacher in the Cherokee schools.

For this book she has provided translations into Cherokee, phonetically and in the syllabary, for a well-known story. The reader can see here the Cherokee language as it appears on the page, with each symbol representing a syllable. This is the system devised by Sequoyah, the only individual in history known to have created a system of written language without being literate himself. The phonetic translation is based on international phonetic symbols; in this system, the letter "v" stands for a short "u" sound with a nasal inflection—"uh" pronounced in the nose.

The Origin of the Milky Way

Some people in the south had a corn mill, in which they pounded the corn into meal, and several mornings when they came to fill it they noticed that some of the meal had been stolen during the night. They examined the ground and found the tracks of a dog, so the next night they watched, and when the dog came from the north and began to eat the meal out of the bowl they sprang out and whipped him. He ran off howling to his home in the north, with the meal dropping from his mouth as he ran, and leaving behind a white trail where now we see the Milky Way, which the Cherokee call to this day Gili uli shv sda nvyi, "where the dog ran" (from James Mooney, *Myths of the Cherokee*).

» Gílí Ulísvdanvyí

ᎩᎵ ᎤᎵᏒᏍᏓᏅᏱ

Tsuganawv iditsa anehi igada yvwi selu asdosdi nunvhne, selu
ᏧᎦᎾᏮ ᎢᏗᏣ ᎠᏁᎯ ᎢᎦᏓ ᏴᏫ ᏎᎷ ᎠᏍᏙᏍᏗ ᏄᏅᏁ, ᏎᎷ

unihsdosdi selu itsa
ᎤᏂᏍᏙᏍᏗ ᏎᎷ ᎢᏣ

nanvnehei, halviyuwalidi dagitsvhvsgv widanilanidohv
ᎾᏅᏁᎮᎢ ᎭᎸ ᎢᏳᏩᎵᏗ ᏓᎩᏥᎲᏍᎬ ᏫᏓᏂᎳᏂᏙᎲ

(selu) anadelohosge
(ᏎᎷ) ᎠᎾᏕᎶᎰᏍᎨ

ganosgida gesv selu ihtsa svnoyi iyvhi. Eladino unigoliyee,
ᎦᏃᏍᎩᏓ ᎨᏒ ᏎᎷ ᎢᏣ ᏒᏃᏱ ᎢᏴᎯ. ᎡᎳᏗᏃ ᎤᏂᎪᎵᏰᎡ,

dunigohe gili
ᏚᏂᎪᎮ ᎩᎵ

dulasinvsdanv, nahiyu sunaleiyv ulisihvsa unagisesdane,
ᏚᎳᏏᏅᏍᏓᏅ, ᎾᎯᏳ ᏑᎾᎴᎢᏴ ᎤᎵᏏᎲᏌ ᎤᎾᎩᏎᏍᏓᏁ,

tsuhyvtsv iditsa diyuloshv
ᏧᏴᏨ ᎢᏗᏣ ᏗᏳᎶᏒ

gili ulutsa, ulenv ulisdayvna selu itsa unvwedv galodvi,
ᎩᎵ ᎤᎷᏣ ᎤᎴᏅ ᎤᎵᏍᏓᏴᎾ ᏎᎷ ᎢᏣ ᎤᏅᏪᏛ ᎦᎶᏛᎢ,

tsunanelugise unilivnilei.
ᏧᎾᏁᎷᎩᏎ ᎤᏂᎵᎥᏂᎴᎢ.

Tsuhyvtsv iditsa tsuwenvshv wulishvsdane wuweluwadise
ᏧᏴᏨ ᎢᏗᏣ ᏧᏪᏅᏒ ᏭᎵᏒᏍᏓᏁ ᏭᏪᎷᏩᏗᏎ

utsewotsehe uhnvsgalv
ᎤᏤᏬᏤᎮ ᎤᏅᏍᎦᎸ

selu ihtsa, wudanvne unega wulosv nasgi goiyv gili ulisvsdanvyi
ᏎᎷ ᎢᏣ, ᏭᏓᏅᏁ ᎤᏁᎦ ᏭᎶᏒ ᎾᏍᎩ ᎪᎢᏴ ᎩᎵ ᎤᎵᏒᏍᏓᏅᏱ

tsawidigowatisgoi,
ᏣᏫᏗᎪᏩᏘᏍᎪᎢ,

nasgi Anitsalagi "gili ulisvsdanvyi" tsanosehoi goiyvhi.
ᎾᏍᎩ ᎠᏂᏣᎳᎩ "ᎩᎵ ᎤᎵᏒᏍᏓᏅᏱ" ᏣᏃᏎᎰ Ꭲ ᎪᎢᏴᎯ.

> Freeman Owle

Freeman Owle was born in 1946 in the Cherokee Indian Hospital on the Qualla Boundary and, like the other storytellers in this book, is a member of the Eastern Band of Cherokee Indians. After graduating from Cherokee High School in 1966, Freeman received a B.S. in social work from Western Carolina University and, in 1978, a master's degree in education. He worked for fourteen years as a schoolteacher in the Cherokee school system. Freeman grew up hearing and learning stories in a traditional way.

"In the middle of the winter, when there was not a whole lot of other things to do, we had the old woodstove, and many times on the cold winter evenings we'd sit down around it. My parents would start telling stories of things that had happened in their lifetime. Parching corn on the old stove, and listening to those stories, and sometimes before bedtime they'd turn to ghost stories. Then I left very quickly to put my head under the cover and try to go to sleep. Yeah, it was a storytelling family. We would hear the family history occasionally and we were sort of expected to remember that."

These stories were shared in English, which is Freeman's first language. Although he has picked up some conversational Cherokee, his parents spoke the language very little. He said, "They understood a whole lot more than they would tell us that they did, for the fear that we would get in trouble at school if we learned the language." In the 1950s, children were expected to learn English, get jobs, and leave the Boundary. But their parents and the children themselves were determined to stay. Many of them became educated and returned to Cherokee. "Home is home for most of the Cherokees, and it's very hard to get us to leave. We have an attachment still to the land and the earth."

After Freeman finished his education, he returned to the Qualla Boundary to teach and to raise a family. He has two grown sons, one in college in Greensboro and another who works as a tribal policeman in Cherokee. He has a young daughter at home. Sharing the Cherokee stories and the Owle family stories with his children is important to Freeman. "I still hang onto the stories and share them with my children and hope that they will share them with theirs. And that's what storytelling is all about."

Like Kathi Littlejohn, Freeman began telling stories publicly through his work as a schoolteacher. "The students liked ghost stories and I started telling ghost stories. I started learning other stories about Cherokee legends, and before I knew it I was telling them to the school; and then they wanted me to go to other classrooms, and then eventually I left the school to tell them on the outside. So I'm telling stories to everybody in the Southeast and the Northeast today. I thoroughly enjoy it."

Freeman has been working as a storyteller and giving workshops on Cherokee culture for a number of years. Although he no longer teaches in the public schools, he feels that, through storytelling, he is still an educator. "I feel like that there is an audience that is very receptive and very open-minded at this point in time, and I feel like my importance in life is to go out and to alleviate some of these beliefs that are just untrue." Freeman tries to correct some popular misconceptions: that Cherokees live in tipis, that they live off money from the government, that they're getting rich from gambling. He wants to show that the Cherokee are people, too—that they've always had feelings, that they've always been religious, and that they were literate and civilized at the time of the Removal in 1838.

Like the other storytellers in this book, Freeman recognizes that there has recently been an increase in interest in Cherokee culture, both on the Qualla Boundary and among the general public. When he was a child, he was considered a mixed-blood because of his Scots-Irish grandfather, and when he and his schoolmates played cowboys and Indians, he ironically had to play the least popular role: the Indian. "When it was cowboys and Indians, the Indians were always bad. And the cowboys always won. The cowboys always wore white hats and never got dirty. So when I went to school I was a minority, I was a mixed blood, a *uneg* [*unaka* is the Cherokee word for white, meaning poplar tree or white person]. And so all the little fullbloods got to be the cowboys, and I had to be the Indian."

But today, that has changed, on the Qualla Boundary and elsewhere. "When I go to schools like Alan B. Rutherford and schools in Statesville last week, that I was in, you know what those little kids want to be? They want to be the Indians. Things are changing." He attributes this in part to the influence of the media and movies like *Dances with Wolves*, in which American Indians are portrayed as human beings and heroes. He also attributes it to a search for cultural identity.

When I asked whether Cherokee families were still telling stories, Freeman replied, "It's hard to answer that question 'cause I don't know really. With television and so many VCR's, I think the two-way interaction has been lost so long that there's a need for it. But people love people, and no matter how many gadgets you invent, eventually it'll come back to the old storytelling from one person to another."

Freeman recognizes that he tells different stories for different audiences, and that traditional storytelling is always evolving and changing. "I try to take the environment and my life growing up there on the reservation and put those things together, and the history that I've studied, and to tell the whole story by adding to it a little bit, putting a little bit of life into it, a little bit more emphasis here and there and draw it out—like the people did many years ago in their own environment, in their own happenings of the day."

Like other storytellers, Freeman sometimes consults printed sources like James Mooney's *Myths of the Cherokee* to find new stories to tell. He feels that these are Cherokee stories, and that they are good stories. Not only that, but a relative of his, Mose Owle, was one of Mooney's sources. "Thank goodness Mooney was here and recorded as many stories as he did. We try to expound on those and make them lifelike and realistic."

In addition to being a gifted storyteller, Freeman is also a stone carver, and the two avocations overlap. "In my carving I can do a conglomeration. And through this conglomeration I can also tell the story. Like "The Magic Lake": you can have a bear that is walking toward a pond of water, and then you can have other animals coming toward the pond of water around the stone carving itself, and so you can actually depict the whole story just through stone."

This combination of physical and oral craft is traditional as well. "Effigy pipes have been found in the tombs and the village sites of years ago, and they're linked to the legends and the stories that the Cherokee people taught," Freeman explains. Effigies were carved for each clan, and each clan had its own stories. Shell gorgets from the Mississippian period (about 500–1500 A.D.) include distinctive motifs that probably relate to stories. During this period, a death mask carved for an individual would reflect the story of his or her life.

When I asked Freeman what he considered the place of storytelling in his life, he said he wanted to be remembered as someone who spread the word of the Cherokee. "Like my carvings, my stories also will, like the stone, will fall into the soil and they will stay there. Stone will not erode away for thousands of years. And I hope that my stories that I've told children across the country will last as long as the stones, because people will always be here."

➤➤

Of the sixteen of Freeman's stories collected here along with an introduction, four are found in Mooney's collection in pretty much the same form ("The Nikwasi Mound," "The Daughter of the Sun," "How the Possum Lost His Tail," and "The Origin of Strawberries"), but Freeman tells them in his own language, with different details, including some historical research on the Nikwasi Mound story. Another four stories are also found in Mooney's collection, though in significantly different versions. "The Magic Lake," "Ganadi, the Great Hunter, and the Wild Boy," "The Story of the Bat," and "The Removed Townhouses," as told by Freeman, include basic differences in plot as well as in details. The other eight folktales and narratives—"Medicine and the Wolf Clan," "The Earth," "Going to Water," "Storytelling," "The Turtle and the Beaver," "The Turtle and

the Raccoon—Stealing Beauty," "The Trail of Tears," and "Corn
Woman Spirit"—are not in Mooney's collection.

The stories were collected at two different sessions. In October
1996, Freeman Owle was invited to tell stories for the public in an
evening sponsored by the Nantahala Hiking Club, held at the Tartan
Hall of the First Presbyterian Church in Franklin. About 150 people
attended, primarily members of the hiking club, who are mostly
retirees, and people from the town of Franklin, including some
families with children. Franklin is built on the site of an ancient
village, Nikwasi, and the Nikwasi Mound has been preserved in the
middle of the town, along the Little Tennessee River.

The last five stories were told by Freeman in an interview setting
at the Qualla Arts and Crafts Co-op in Cherokee, North Carolina, on
a rainy morning in the spring of 1996. These are stories that Freeman also tells in his public performances, but they were not among
the ones he told on the evening in Franklin. "The Origin of Strawberries," "Corn Woman Spirit," "The Story of the Bat," "Ganadi, the
Great Hunter, and the Wild Boy," and "The Removed Townhouses"
are all what we might call classic myths for the Cherokee. Here Freeman also discusses his thoughts on the meanings of these stories.

➤➤ Introduction to the Nantahala Hiking Club Gathering

Thank you very much for inviting me here tonight.
Can everyone hear fine?
My name is Freeman Owle,
I'm from Cherokee, North Carolina,
   born and reared on the Cherokee Indian Reservation.
In 1946,
   many of you may remember,
   and maybe not,
   the A-models coming over the Smokies,
   people going up into the bear jams
   and the old cars overheating.
People backing up for miles,
   and Roosevelt on top of the mountain

when they dedicated the Blue Ridge Parkway.
They said something to the effect that:
>"Look what we made out of this land, that for so long belonged
>>to the savages,"
>and I think they still have it inscribed into the rocks
>up on top of Clingman's Dome.
I'm not quite so sure that those people were the savages
>that Roosevelt may have thought that they were.
Coming down from the hills
>and fighting with their Iroquois brother over some argument,
>point of view or something,
>they moved southward.
They moved into the Cumberland Mountains.
But the Iroquois brother still said,
>"That's not far enough,"
>and the Tsa-la-gi,
>they called themselves Tsa-la-gi,
>moved a little bit farther into Kentucky and Tennessee,
>and eventually the Iroquois brother thought they'd moved far
>>enough away.
I can imagine many times
>the land and the landscape that they came upon,
>a land of virgin timber,
>a land with a stream so crystal-clear
>you could count every pebble in the bottom of the stream.
A land where the wild turkey walked leisurely,
>and a land where deer were jumping from behind almost every
>>bush.
Coming down
>into the hills and the valleys of the Oconaluftee,
>the Tuckaseegee,
>and the Tennessee,
>they began to look for a place to live.
Hearing drumbeats somewhere in the distance,
>they realized that they were not the only people here.
They began to come out and to part the leaves
>and look out into the valleys of Nikwasi.
Seeing people walking in this flat field down here below,

seeing a large mound of dirt with buildings on top of it,
    they realized they were not the first people to arrive in this area.
They came to this place called Nikwasi,
    and they met the people who lived here,
    who were blond-headed and blue-eyed.
Thousands and thousands of years before Leif Erickson and the
        Vikings,
    thousands of years before the settlers came,
    there were peoples with blond hair and blue eyes already here.
James Mooney may tell you,
    in his writings of Cherokee myths and legends and sacred
        formulas,
    that the Cherokees annihilated these people
    and they were no more.
I truly believe
    that the Cherokees intermarried with these people,
    and they are still here.
You go to Cherokee, North Carolina, today,
    and you see those folks with Eskimo-type facial features,
    and you'll also see those with the South American–type features.
And in Robbinsville, North Carolina, in a little place called
        Snowbird,
    you can still see those real dark-skinned Cherokees,
    and every now and then
    you'll see one with a reddish tint in their hair and blue eyes.
The people got along well together because they loved the earth.
And you people who hike—
    at least you have got to the point in your lives
    when you can go out into the forest,
    and you don't have to run through the forest
    to get from one end to the other.
You may have had to do that for a lifetime.
But it's now a time to slow down
    and listen to the stream as it gurgles by,
    it's time to slow down
    and listen to the call of the birds and see if you can identify it,
    it's time to sometimes take your shoes off,
    and, like a little child,

to go and splash in the waters of the Tennessee or the Nantahala.
Once you lose that childlikeness,
    then you've lost life.
The Cherokee people believe that everything is connected,
    everything that is living is a part of the great cycle,
    and we as people, human beings, are part of that great cycle also.
Society may take you by the throat and strangle you
    to the point that you feel like you must gain success.
I grew up on the Cherokee reservation
    in the time of 1946,
    when the tourists began to come,
    and the Cherokees' culture began to die and began to be
        removed,
    and people were asked and forced out upon the streets
    because it was role-expectation theory
    that you go out and you put on the Sioux headdress,
    and you stand in front of a Sioux tipi,
    and those peoples coming along
    would stand there and have their pictures taken with you—
    that's what they expected us to be.
The Cherokee people were woodland farmers,
    and they farmed for a living for twenty or thirty thousand years.
They had no need to take down their house
    and follow the buffalo herd
    because the buffalo that were here were woodland buffalo
    that stood very, very tall, usually traveled in pairs of two.
The Cherokees have made up many, many stories
    as they've lived in these valleys.
And I'm respectful of Franklin, North Carolina.
I know that sometimes you're under a lot of controversy and
        discussion.
You are one of the very few areas that has protected your mound,
    that is located within your village.
I as an individual, and as a member of the Eastern Band of the
        Cherokees,
    commend you for this.
It's a beautiful mound.
And one of the very few, that I know of, that's still intact.

There are stories behind this,
>   because when the Cherokees farmed,
>   they had enough food that they were able to store their food for
>   the winter,
>   and then when the cold winters came
>   they were able to sit down in front of the fires built in those old
>   cabins
>   and to tell stories.
One of the ones they tell is about Nikwasi.

» The Nikwasi Mound

Nikwasi was down on the valley of the Tennessee,
>   and all of a sudden the Creeks began to come up and attack
>   and threaten to destroy the village of Nikwasi.
The Cherokee people rallied,
>   they came to protect the village,
>   but over and over again the Creeks came in greater numbers,
>   and eventually the Cherokees were losing, very badly.
And they'd almost given up,
>   when all of a sudden the mound of Nikwasi opened up,
>   and little soldiers began to march out of this mound by the
>   thousands.
And so they go out and they defeat the Creeks,
>   and like in biblical times
>   they kill all of the Creeks except for one.
And he goes back and tells the other Creek brothers and sisters,
>   "Never ever mess with the village of Nikwasi,
>   because they have spirit people who protect it."
And never again
>   was this village attacked by the Creeks.
It was during the Civil War time
>   that the Yankee soldiers came down from the north,
>   and they were camped out
>   and ready to come down and to burn
>   the little town of Franklin, North Carolina.
They sent scouts down to Franklin, North Carolina,
>   and the scouts went back telling their commanding officer,

"You can't attack Franklin, North Carolina.
    It is heavily guarded, there's soldiers on every corner."
And the soldiers went around,
    toward Atlanta, Georgia, and burned everything in the path.
But Franklin, North Carolina, was not touched.
And then the history and the reality was
    that every able fighting person left Franklin
    to fight in the Civil War.
There were no men here.
The old Cherokees say it was the Nunnehi, the Little People,
    that again protected
    Franklin, North Carolina.

» Medicine and the Wolf Clan

In the old days,
    it's said,
    that back in the very, very beginning times,
    after the villages were built,
    it was an old man who came walking out of the woods,
    and he had sores all over his body,
    and he came down to the clans of the Cherokee,
    and he said to the first woman in charge of the first clan,
    "Would you take me in and make me well?"
And she said,
    "Oh, you look so terrible, we don't know how to make you well.
    Go away."
The man goes down to another clan of the Cherokee,
    it could have been the Blue Clan,
    and the woman comes out and says,
    "We have children here.
    Don't, don't bother us, please go away."
Again and again
    he's turned away from these villages,
    and eventually he comes to the Wolf Clan of the Cherokee.
All the terrible sores on his body,
    and he says to the woman of the Wolf Clan,
    "Will you bring me in and make me well?"

She says,
    "I don't know what to do for you.
    But if you'll come in,
    we will lay you down upon the bed,
    and we will do everything we possibly can
    to make you better."
He went in,
    and he lay down upon the bed,
    and he sent her out to the forest the first day and said,
    "Get the bark of the cherry tree and bring it back and make tea to
        let me drink."
And she did.
And his cold went away.
    "Go back to the willow tree
    and get some bark and make it into a poultice
    and wring it and put it upon my sores."
And she did.
And the sores went away.
Again and again for a long time
    he sent her into the forest,
    telling her every time a certain cure for a certain ailment.
After a while
    he was completely healed.
Then one day he got up from the bed and said,
    "Since you were good to me,
    I have taught you, the women of the Wolf Clan,
    all the cures of the forest.
    And from this day forward,
    you, the women of the Wolf Clan,
    will be the doctors of the communities and the reservations."

›› The Earth

So the Cherokee people still believe that the earth has a lot to give.
They still believe that it's important to take care of the waters,
    to preserve the air,
    to preserve the forest,
    to preserve the life of people themselves.

When I was a child growing up on the reservation,
  it was not beyond the times of beauty.
It was a time early in the morning,
   when my father would awaken me
   and tell me that it was time to go to the forest.
We would get up before daylight and head to the mountaintop.
As we walked, I wondered why.
As I walked, I would sometimes place my foot upon a twig,
   and it would break and snap,
   and he would turn very quietly and say, "Shh."
I would place my feet more carefully,
   and after a while
   I noticed that I was able to place them by feeling where they
      were going,
   without making a sound.
We walked in the darkness for a long time and finally came to a
      clearing,
   and I noticed the beautiful stars in the sky early that morning.
And he said,
   "Sit down."
I sat down upon the ground,
   and I began to look at the beautiful heavens,
   and after a while I began to hear noises, all around.
And he said,
   "Be quiet."
There was a noise off to the left,
   then a noise in the front,
   and then the leaves were rattling in the trees up to the right,
   but I remained still.
After a while,
   the rays of sunlight began to take over the skies,
   and the stars disappear.
The rays of sun revealed to me
   that off on the right were squirrels jumping in the hickory nut
      trees,
   revealed to me
   that in front of me in the forest there was a deer, with its baby,

and off to the left the grouse was shuffling in the leaves with
    baby chicks.
And no sooner had the sun come,
    than my father said,
    "We're ready to go."
We got up from the clearing,
    and we walked out of the forest,
    and in my mind was a question of
    why that we had done this.
But after I returned home,
    he told me,
    "What have you learned?"
I said,
    "I've learned, Father, that if you're quiet enough,
    still enough, long enough,
    that you become part of nature."
And he said,
    "You've learned well, son."
He loved the forest.
He loved to tell the stories of the Cherokees.
And one of the ones he told me many times was the story of the
    magic lake.

❯❯ The Magic Lake

He said
    there was a young lad walking in the forest one day.
I remember these stories because a lot of times at night,
    we were sitting in front of an old wood heater—
    all nine of my brothers and sisters and I—
    having corn.
And I don't know if you've ever done this or not,
    but you'd take a little bit of oil and put it into a frying pan,
    and you'd put it on that very hot stove and put kernels of corn
        in it.
They didn't pop but they parched.
Then after a while

when they got done you could crunch those,
and listen to the stories.
And this young Cherokee boy was walking in the woods,
and he saw droplets of blood upon the leaves,
and he began to follow those
because he was concerned with something being hurt,
because all the animals were important.
He followed them up the hillside
and eventually came upon a small bear cub
who had been wounded, and his leg was bleeding.
And up the hill he went, following it,
and it would stumble and fall,
and make its way to its feet again,
and it was struggling, going in one direction,
to the great mountain that the Cherokees call Shakonige,
which is the Blue Mountain
or, today, Clingman's Dome.
And it was a sacred mountain to the Cherokee
and a very special place.
Eventually nightfall came and the bear lay down.
The young man stayed close by that night,
and early in the next morning
the little cub again got up
to go up to the top of the mountain,
and this time made it to the top.
And the fog was covering everything
except for the very peaks of the mountains.
The little cub goes over, and it jumps into the fog.
And the young man says,
"Surely he's gone now."
But all of a sudden
the fog turns to water,
and the little bear begins to swim.
He swims out a ways,
and then he comes back,
and when he gets out of the water,
his leg is completely healed.
And the young man is very confused.

He looks,
 and a duck swims in the water with a broken wing,
 and his wing is made well.
And animals are coming from all directions
 and coming to the water,
 and they're swimming and being healed.
He looks up at the Great Spirit,
 and he says,
 "I don't understand."
The Great Spirit says,
 "Go back and tell your brothers and sisters the Cherokee,
 if they love me,
 if they love all their brothers and sisters,
 and if they love the animals of the earth,
 when they grow old and sick,
 they too can come to a magic lake and be made well again."

This was a belief that was "savage."

▸▸ Going to Water

The same "savage" would go down to the waters of the Tennessee,
 right down here,
 early in the morning every morning,
 wade out waist deep,
 take the waters of the river and throw it up over his head.
And say,
 "Wash away any thoughts or feelings
 that may hinder me from being closer to my God.
 Take away any thoughts or feelings
 that may hinder me from being closer to all my brothers and
    sisters on the earth,
 and the animals of the earth."
And they would wash themselves
 and cleanse themselves
 every morning,
 and then they would walk out of the water.
And you see many people using crystals today,

but the only use I know—
the Cherokee had pure crystal.
They would hold it in front of the individual,
    and if he saw himself upside down in it,
        he had to go back into the water and do the same thing over
            again.
But if he was upright, he was cleansed, and free to go about his
            daily work.
Those people loved the earth.

➤➤ The Daughter of the Sun

The daughter of the Sun was another legend the Cherokees told.
And this one is not told as much,
    but it has a lot of very interesting meanings and values to teach,
    and it's unusual that the Sun would be a woman.
The Sun and her daughter the Moon are crossing the sky.
And one day the Sun looked down and noticed
    that all the people were looking at her rather squinch-eyed
    and with ugly faces every time they looked at her
    because of her great brightness.
So the Sun got very angry
    and said that she didn't like for people to look at her like that.
    And the Cherokees were making fun of her
    by making faces at her.
And she got very angry,
    and she began to increase her heat
    coming down upon the earth.
And the people were so hot their crops began to dry up,
    and they began to pray to the Great Spirit
    to get the Sun to stop making it so hot.
And it continued on.
So they began to turn to their medicine people,
    and they went to this old medicine man,
    and he said,
    "Well, we can talk to the Sun,
    and we can sing to her,
    and see if we can get her to calm down

and lessen her heat."
So they began to sing to the Sun.
But of course when they looked at her
    their faces were still all squinched and drawn.
And she was not very happy,
    and she didn't like the music,
      so she made it even hotter.
And the streams began to dry up,
    and the trees began to die,
    and the crops they planted wouldn't even come up,
    so the Cherokees had real problems.
And they decided, through their medicine people,
    that they would kill the Sun.
And so the medicine man changed a person into a rattlesnake,
    and he was supposed to go up into the heavens
    and find his way to where the Sun crossed the sky,
    and when she went in to visit her daughter the Moon,
    the next morning when the Sun came out,
    the rattlesnake was to bite her and kill her.
So sure enough,
    he made his way into the heavens
    and found the house of the Moon,
    and he sat out by the doorway
    and waited for the Sun to come out.
And she came out that morning,
    and she came out so quickly
    that he struck—
    and she was so bright,
    and he missed.
So he came back to the earth
    and told the medicine people what had happened.
So they were very upset with him
    and told him that the next day they would send a copperhead.
So the copperhead went up and he hid by the doorway,
    and the Sun came out,
    and he struck—
    and he was to try to get her before she came out—
    and he struck too soon

and missed,
and the Sun went on its way.
So the next day they sent both of them up
and told them that they would *have* to kill the Sun,
that they would both strike
just before she came out,
as soon as the door was open, they would strike.
And sure enough, the door opened that morning,
and they struck,
and all of a sudden they hit something
and looked,
and it fell to the ground,
and it was the daughter of the Sun.
The Moon had come up that day.
And so they were very upset.
And when the Sun saw this,
she was very, very angry,
and she began to burn
and even set fires on the earth with her great heat.
The people were digging into the earth trying to save themselves.
And the rattlesnake came back, and the copperhead,
and they changed themselves back into people,
and they told the people what had happened.
So the medicine man said the only way they could make things
right
would be to go to the land of the dead.
Take seven sourwood sticks
and find the daughter of the Sun
dancing in the great circle of the dead,
and when she came around
they would touch her
seven times
with those sticks,
and she would fall down asleep,
and they would put her into a great basket
and carry her back to the land of the Cherokee.
But the medicine man said,
"Under no conditions should you open the basket

even just a little bit."
So they had gone to the land of the dead;
    after many, many days' journey
    and great problems finding their way there,
    they finally made it.
And sure enough,
    there was that great circle of death
    where the people were dancing,
    and they saw the daughter of the Sun.
She danced around to where they were,
    and they touched her the first time,
    and seven times they touched her
    with those sourwood sticks,
    and she didn't even know it.
On the seventh time she fell to the ground.
They picked her up and put her in the basket
    and started their long journey back to the land of the Cherokee.
On the way back, the daughter of the Sun began to talk
    in the basket.
Said she was getting very warm inside,
    and would they please open it just a little bit.
But they wouldn't do that;
    they remembered their instructions.
After a while she began to say she was getting thirsty,
    and then they ignored that.
Then she said she was hungry,
    and they sort of thought,
        "Well, if we let her starve to death, we'll really be in trouble,"
    and they were tempted to open the basket,
    but they didn't.
After a while she began to say
    in a very weak voice,
    "I'm hungry
    and I'm smothering to death.
    I need air."
So one of the people in the group decided they could open it
    just a little bit
    to give her some air.

When they opened it
   there was a red light,
     a flittering coming out of the basket,
   and it went off into the forest.
And they closed it back real quickly
   and said,
   "Well, we can't do that.
   We better follow instructions."
They carried the big basket
   all the way back to the village,
   and when they got there,
   immediately the medicine man knew they'd opened the basket.
So when he looked inside he was very angry
   because there was nothing inside at all.
They began to wail in their great sadness.
They looked outside, and the Sun was scorching the earth.
All of a sudden they noticed that it began to cool off a little bit.
They looked out, and the lady Sun was smiling.
And they listened,
   and they heard this sound
   of a beautiful song
   coming from a bird in the bush.
They looked over to the bush,
   and there was
   a beautiful redbird.
And as it sang,
   the Sun smiled,
   and the heat decreased.
They then knew that the redbird
   was the daughter of the Sun.
From that day forward,
   the Sun has been good to the Cherokee people.

›› How the Possum Lost His Tail

Many stories were told.
Many stories were teaching stories.
The old story of possum was told

to keep children from bragging and boasting.
The possum was a beautiful creature, but he didn't know that.
And one day he was walking out beside the waters
    and looked into the very, very still waters and saw a reflection of
        himself
    and realized that his tail was big and fluffy and beautiful and
        many, many colors.
So he began to admire himself,
    and he walked by that water all day long
    until the wind began to blow.
And then he walked away
    and began to boast and brag to the other animals in the forest.
And early every morning he was out
    in the center of the forest
    and waking all the animals up
    to see how beautiful his tail was that day.
Many, many days passed,
    and they began to get tired of it—
    of his boasting and bragging—
    because they knew he was beautiful.
And the fox and the cricket got so tired of it
    that they made a plan to put an end to it.
They had a contest set up in the squaregrounds of the Cherokee the
        next day
    and invited Mr. Possum to come down and participate,
    because it was a contest to see who had the most beautiful tail.
And sure, he would do that, he knew he would win, and that
        would be fine.
But they coaxed him into going with them that night
    to comb and brush his tail.
And when he went into the cave of the fox,
    they began to brush his tail and groom it,
    and he began to get a little sleepy.
And as he began to get sleepy,
    they brushed a little faster,
    and soon Mr. Possum was fast asleep.
The cricket, being the creature that he is, began to chew,
    and he chewed *every* hair off the possum's tail.

Well, it was not a very pretty tail at that time,
   and they tied it up with a piece of deerskin
   and tied a beautiful bow on the end of it.
And early next morning when the possum awakened, he said,
   "What did you do to my tail?"
   being very upset.
And they said, "Oh, we combed and brushed it so beautifully
   that we felt like we had to wrap it up
   so it would not get messed up."
And so he was in agreement to that,
   and he bounced on off to the squaregrounds.
And the animals began to go across the stage.
And you had the skunk
   with his beautiful black tail
   with a white streak down the middle.
And of course he didn't smell very good,
   but all the people were pleased,
   at a distance.
And the other animals crossed the stage,
   the squirrel,
   and the red fox
   with his big, beautiful orange tail with the black spot on the end.
The possum couldn't wait any longer,
   and he began to get antsy.
So he jumped up on the stage
   and he said,
   "It's my time, we need to get this thing settled."
So he said,
   "Take the thing off my tail."
And when they take it off,
   all the animals, and all the people in the audience
   began to roll and laugh and giggle.
And he looks back at his tail,
   and he sees what they're laughing about.
He has the most ugly,
   rat-looking tail
   that he's ever seen in his life.
And first he begins to snarl and spit

and become very angry.
But after a little while they laugh again
    and he can't stand it anymore,
    and he rolls over on his back and he plays dead.
The old possum boasted too much.
And if you go out today
    and find him in your trash cans,
    you will see that he begins to snarl like he's going to tear you to
        pieces.
And if you poke him with a little stick,
    he'll remember
    that he boasted too much.
And he'll roll over onto his back
    with all four feet sticking into the air.
And you can pick him up by the tail
    and carry him back into the forest.
So the teaching of the Cherokee possum story is:
You should let other people
    tell you that you're beautiful.
Don't go around telling everyone else
    that you are.
Okay?

➡ Storytelling

As I go across the country telling stories to children,
    you can look back and you see their eyes are wide open,
    and you see their little mouths open up wide.
And sometimes the little boys especially
    look like they're about ready to come up out of their seats.
Storytelling is something that is a two-way interaction:
    I'm looking at you, I'm looking at your face,
    and you're looking at me, and we're interacting.
Children of today get in front of a TV,
    turn on the knob,
    and it's only one-way.
They have no input,
    they have no identity,

they have no place,
  and they have no one there with them.
Storytelling is important—
  and I listened,
  and I would have listened
  even without the popcorn and the parched corn.

» The Turtle and the Beaver

But the stories—of the turtle, for example.
This turtle was living in the lake,
  and he had a pole that came up out of the water.
And that pole just came up at a beautiful slant.
And he would crawl up on that pole,
  after eating as many little minnows as he wanted,
  and sun himself when he got cool.
He got too hot,
  he could climb right off the end of it.
And there was a beautiful tree up on the bank,
  and he would get under the shade tree
  and cool himself down if he got too hot.
He had everything he wanted.
One fall of the year
  he went down to the waters.
It was getting cold,
  and he dived deeply into the water
  and buried himself in the mud.
And he slept very comfortably that winter.
Too much so, I imagine,
  because when the spring currents began to come,
  and the thunder and the lightning shook the earth,
  he was supposed to awaken.
But he pushed "snooze,"
  like some of us may do.
And he stayed in there just a little longer.
And the earth began to really tremble,
  and when he awakened and came to the top,

he noticed
that it was taking him a little bit longer to get to the surface.
He noticed
that his tree that was slanted just right
was completely submerged.
He went on to the top as fast as he could,
and oh, it was deep.
He got up there,
and he looked up,
and his shade tree—
there was nothing there but a pile of shavings and a stump.
He looked down to the head of the waters,
and sure enough,
there was a whole pile of trees over the front of the lake there,
and it had been dammed up.
And he saw this creature with a big black head,
and it was swimming toward him with two or three
companions.
And he had a big flat tail,
and he would slap it in the water,
and he looked so vicious.
He came up to the turtle and said,
"Mr. Turtle, this is my lake. You will have to leave."
The turtle says,
"Oh no, I've been here forever, this has always been my home.
I do not intend to leave."
The beaver says,
"My brothers and sisters and I
will chew your shell off and throw you over the dam if you don't
leave."
Mr. Turtle looked at him and said,
"Oh, we don't have to fight.
We'll have a contest.
We'll swim to the other side of the lake, and the winner will take
all."
So the beavers were really pleased.
They knew how fast they could swim.

They knew how slow the turtle was, and they said, "Fine."
The turtle says,
    "Wait a minute, though, I'll even give you a head start, Mr.
        Beaver.
    I'm really a fast swimmer, so you can have a head start,
    and that will give you a fair chance,"
And the beaver said, "Fine."
Out they took off swimming across the lake
    and all of a sudden, sure enough,
    the beaver was running off and leaving the turtle.
But the turtle reached out his long neck,
    and he bit into the beaver's tail.
With that beak it hurt,
    and the beaver began to swing his tail back and forth in pain,
    and he thought,
    "I can't shake that turtle, but I can swim to the other side and I
        can win.
    So he'll be back there."
And he swam toward the other side as fast as he could.
Before he got to the other side,
    the turtle saw he was getting close,
    so the turtle bit down with all his might,
    and the beaver screamed,
    and he threw his tail up in the air.
Just at the top of the arc,
    the turtle lets go.
He lands on the shore
    in front of the beaver.
He said,
    "Mr. Beaver, I told you I was a fast swimmer."

I tell the boys and girls in school
    that there's always an opportunity to fight.
But first
    there's always an opportunity
    to outsmart the individual who's going against you.
And it's the easier way of doing things, sometimes.

>> The Turtle and the Raccoon
—Stealing Beauty

This turtle—
    the water went down,
    the beavers had to leave—
    he was out on his beautiful little log again and sunning himself.
And the raccoon came down and said,
    "Mr. Turtle, do you know that you have beautiful rings on your
        neck?"
And turtle said,
    "No I didn't know that."
He said,
    "They really are beautiful. Could I touch one of those rings?
        Please, Mr. Turtle?"
And you know people like this, too:
    "Please, please, please, please,"
    and they go on and on and on and on
    until eventually,
    "You may touch one ring
    if you'll go away and leave me alone."
He touched one ring,
    and his little paw began to glow a beautiful bright yellow.
And he said,
    "Mr. Turtle, could I wear one of those rings on my tail?"
And the old turtle finally said,
    "Yes, you can wear a ring on your tail if you'll go away."
And he gave him the yellow one.
He put it on his tail.
And that raccoon was beautiful.
The people in the forest, they all began to brag on him.
And he came back, and he said,
    "Mr. Turtle, I promise to leave you alone
    if you'll let me wear all seven rings on my tail."
And the turtle eventually decided
    that he could wear all seven rings on his tail,
    if he'd give them right back to him.

And the turtle says,
    "Give them back to me."
The raccoon says,
    "Could I go over by the poplar tree
    and you tell me how I look?"
And sure enough, he goes over by the poplar tree
    and says, "How do I look?"
And all the animals say,
    "You're beautiful."
And the turtle says,
    "Bring them back to me, please."
And the old raccoon runs up the tree.
The turtle crawls over fast as he can,
    and he says,
    "Give me my rings back, please."
The old raccoon says,
    "If you want them back, they're up here.
    You'll have to come and get them."
Of course,
    turtles don't climb very well.
He waited until dark came,
    and he still didn't have his rings back.
So he crawled away
    and buried himself deep in the mud for a long, long time.
That raccoon sat up in that tree that night
    smiling from ear to ear.
And all the animals in the forest were calling
    and telling him how beautiful he was.
He went to sleep smiling that night,
    but when he awakened the next morning,
    he looked back at his tail,
    and all of those beautiful rings had disappeared.
And all he has today
    is seven black rings on his tail.
If we go out, as young people—
    and you may see someone in another grade as a young student—
    you may want to be like this person.
You may

walk like him,
talk like him,
dress like him—or her.
But if you try to steal someone else's beauty,
    you'll awaken one morning,
    and it will all have faded away.
Each and every one of us is a very special and beautiful person.
We were born one of a kind.
Never again will there be a person like you in this world,
    and never before has there been.
Your fingerprints are proof of that.
They're all different.
So we're all very, very special.

>> The Trail of Tears

I found that out as I was growing up,
    and my parents began to tell me this story of the Trail of Tears.
And you look at me and you say,
    "Well, he's probably as much Scots-Irish as I am."
Yes, I am.
But I am Ooguku tsiskayi Tsalagi ashkaya.
My name is Owle, I live in Birdtown,
    and I happened to grow up on the reservation.
Sort of like a little story that Marsha was reading to our daughter
            last night
    about the zebra.
Says, "Are you white with black stripes or black with white
            stripes?"
Are you Scots-Irish with Indian, or Indian with Scots-Irish?
I don't know, I really don't.
All I know is I'm different from anyone who's ever lived,
    and different than anyone who ever will.
And my fingerprints are different, so I must be special.
They told me that
    my family was, in 1838, in a log cabin near Murphy, North
            Carolina.
And all of a sudden,

someone was banging on the door
   early that morning.
And they opened up the door and they looked out,
   and fifty Georgia soldiers were standing in the yard.
They said,
   "Come out of the cabin."
And when my great-grandfather—
   I'll just call him grandfather—
   did,
   they burned the cabin to the ground.
He and his wife and small baby were taken to Murphy, North
       Carolina,
   put into a stockade,
   stayed there for six weeks.
There was no roof, only a line of poles
   encircling the stockade.
They say that
   the mud was deep,
   there wasn't much food,
   no one had anything to cover themselves with,
   but the baby survived because the mother was feeding it.
Early one morning,
   on that October morning
   when the frost was heavy
   and the ground was frozen hard enough for wagons to travel,
   General Winfield Scott began to march the people out of this fort.
So he marched them across the frozen ground
   and across the Santeetlah Mountains
   into Tennessee.
There was a woman by the name of Martha Ross,
   Scots-Irish and Cherokee.
She had a beautiful coat,
   and she began to look, late that night,
   and the rain was coming down, and it was cold,
   and she heard a baby crying.
She went to the sound of the baby and found the child
   very cold
   and wet—

it had pneumonia.
She covered the child with her coat,
    and two days later she died of pneumonia herself.
It is people like this
    who have made contributions to the Cherokee society.
It is people like the people of North Carolina
    who allowed those people living in North Carolina to remain
            there.
The history is written,
    the history says
    that North Carolina did not remove its Cherokees.
They were called the Oconaluftee Cherokees.
And you go see *Unto These Hills*, it doesn't mention this.
But they didn't make them leave.
The other fifteen thousand began to march on toward Oklahoma.
When they got to the Mississippi, they asked my grandfather
    if he would count the Cherokees who crossed the river.
And he said,
    "Yes, I will."
But he told his wife in Cherokee,
    "Go hide in the cane brake and take the baby with you.
    And I will tell them you're here.
    And we'll go back home."
So he counted the Cherokees as they crossed the flatboat across the
            Mississippi,
    and he told the soldiers,
    "All the Cherokees are accounted for."
And they said,
    "Are you sure?
    Go back to the river and check again."
And this was what he wanted,
    and he goes back to the river,
    and he looks into the bushes and the brush,
    and all of a sudden he leaps into the water.
They come running behind, and they shoot many times into the
            water.
They look into the black, swirling waters of the Mississippi,
    and this Cherokee doesn't surface.

So—for a long time.
And they give him up as being dead.
He's breathing through a reed all this time.
And after he gives the soldiers time enough to go away,
    he comes up and he swims back
    across the Mississippi.
He looks for his wife on the other side,
    and—she heard the gunshots.
She ran
    with the baby in her arms,
    she would run all night long,
    and then find a briar patch to sleep in in the daytime,
    or a farmer's haystack.
Took her several weeks to get back home,
    but she came on back to the old burned-out cabin site
    because that's all she knew as home.
She waited there week after week,
    and her husband didn't return.
She went down to the village,
    to the Scots-Irish settlers,
    and they gladly gave her food.
And they were feeding those Cherokees
    that were hiding in the mountains.
If the North Carolina people had been caught by the Georgia guard
    handing out food to the Cherokees,
    they too would have lost their land and been put in prison
    as Cherokee sympathizers.
But the Scots-Irish people were feeding her
    one morning, a year later,
    when she heard a noise up on the hill,
    and she looked and there was someone coming.
And so she ran and hid with the baby.
And after a while it was her husband
    coming out of the woods.
They were reunited,
    and we still live
    in a little place where they came and rebought with their own
        money

called Birdtown.
And the reason they were able to rebuy it was:
    there was a wagon train coming through here,
    and it had a little baby on it—
    a little white child
    who was very sick.
And the parents were smart enough to say,
    "If we go on with this child, it's going to die."
And they said—
    have you ever heard the term, "Give it to the Indians"?
    They gave the child to the Indians.
Chief Yonaguska made the child better.
His name was William Holland Thomas.
Will Thomas was already a citizen of the United States,
    and the Cherokees could go and buy up land
    and put it in this child's name
    by the thousands of acres,
    and we are still here.
But in the early 1920s
    my grandfather, Solomon Owle,
    was living in this little place called Birdtown
    and paying his taxes to Swain County,
    and I think was a good citizen.
The federal government looked down and said,
    "This can't be.
    This bunch of savages are not supposed to be able to take care of
        themselves."
And they came down and took the deeds away from these people
    and set up what they called the Qualla Indian Boundary.
They couldn't call it a reservation
    because a reservation is land that is given to the Indians,
    and the Indians are forced upon it.
This land was bought back
    under Will Thomas's name—
    see, it's not a reservation
    it's a little different.
You know, I came here tonight to tell you
    that the Cherokee people don't really hold any hatred

or animosity in their heart
for those things that happened in the past.
We can take our hats off to the past,
    but as one great gentleman said,
    "We should take our shirts off to the future."
The reason the Cherokee people survived
    is because they loved their neighbors
    and were good neighbors.
The Cherokees of today
    still welcome even all the visitors in the '41 Chevys
    and the '40 Ford coupes
    and the bears and everything—
    they were glad to see the tourists come.
And we're glad to see the tourists come, even today.

» The Origin of Strawberries

One of the ones that I like to tell to people here—
    and through my storytelling
    I've tried to sort of analyze what the stories really meant
    when they were presented to the children back in the old times.
And I found specifically that stories
    like the story of the creation of strawberries
    have special meanings, and I'll try to convey that.
They say once there was a man who,
    in this matrilineal society,
    his wife had told him to go out and kill a deer that day.
And he went out with good intentions of bringing back a deer,
    because her family was coming that evening to have dinner with
        them,
    and the grandmother, her mother, was a very important person
        in that society.
So he went out that day and he was looking for a deer,
    preferably the best one he could find.
And he happened to come across a fellow who had fallen into a
        ravine,
    and his leg was broken,
    and so he went down in the ravine and helped him out

 and carried him back to his village,
  and by the time he made it back to the village,
  it was very late in the day.
So he went back to the forest real quickly and started to hunt.
And by that time all of the deer had gone in and he couldn't find
   one.
So he came back to his village where his wife was living.
And she saw him coming on the hillside.
And he didn't have a deer.
So she got very angry,
 and she began to throw things,
 and she ran away out of the village and left
 and went back toward her own village, her mother's village.
And he came back
 and was praying to the Great Spirit
 and was telling him that he would like for the Great Spirit to
   slow her down,
 so he could tell her what happened that day
 and the reason for him not bringing the deer back.
She was moving very quickly, and the Great Spirit said that he
   would.
So he began to put beautiful flowers in her path.
And this didn't slow her down at all,
 she just kept right on running
 as fast as she could go.
And so he began to put fruit trees in her path,
 and she would go around them
 and was not even interested in the fruit.
So the Great Spirit said that he would have to put something in the
   path
 that smelled delicious,
 that looked beautiful to the eye,
 and tasted very, very good.
So he put this little plant right down near her feet,
 because she was angry and looking down.
And she saw these beautiful little white flowers,
 and then began to see a red fruit on the ground.
Then eventually she smelled it, and it was wonderful.

And then she began to pick some of them and taste them,
    and they were so good that she sat down in the middle of the
        patch.
And the young man caught up with her
    while she was eating the strawberries,
    and he apologized to her
    and told her what had happened.
So she realized that she had left in anger
    and went on back to the village.
I think this is a teaching to the children
    that we shouldn't in the heat of anger
    jump up and run away
    and make real drastic decisions or actions at that point.
And so each and every story had a real reason for it.
The Cherokees did not have schools,
    so they had to tell stories to teach their children.

›› Corn Woman Spírit

Another story that gives some respect to the women in the tribe—
    and I mentioned that it is a matrilineal society.
There's a story of the Corn Woman.
And she is a spirit that is sent down from heaven every year
    to come and walk in the fields of the Cherokee.
And when she walked in the fields
    the corn began to grow,
    and it grew tall and beautiful.
And the Cherokee corn is a corn that is very, very special,
    because it is a corn that has ten rows of kernels on it.
And most other ears have thirteen,
    that we are familiar with today.
So the Cherokee corn will grow ten, almost ten feet tall,
    and on those stalks it will have three or four ears of corn,
    where most [other kinds of] stalks have one or two,
    and it's beautiful in color.
It's all the colors of the rainbow.
And many people ask, "How did you paint that?"
And the Cherokees ate it.

It's a very good corn.
Anyway, this Corn Woman would walk in the fields,
    and the corn would grow beautifully.
One year they planted their corn
    and had gone out to watch it come up,
    and it didn't come up.
And they waited a week,
    and then two weeks,
    and it still hadn't come up.
So they prayed to the Great Spirit
    and asked where the Corn Woman Spirit was.
And he said that he had sent her down two weeks before,
    and she was missing, evidently.
And so the people began to look.
And they looked all over the earth known to them at that time,
    and they couldn't find her.
So they began to ask the animal kingdom
    if they would help search for her.
So all the animals were searching for this beautiful Corn Woman
        Spirit
    when all of a sudden the raven dived down into a dark cave
    and was looking for her.
And he found her in the bottom of the cave, all tied up.
She was captured and prisoner
    of the evil spirit Hunger.
And he was dancing around her and laughing,
    knowing very well that if she didn't get out,
    that the Cherokee people would starve the coming winter.
So the raven went back and reported to the people
    that he had found the Corn Woman Spirit.
And they told the raven
    that only he and his family could get her free.
So they told him to go down into the cave
    and perch on the ledges
    and hide from the evil spirit,
    and he did.
He took all of his brothers and sisters into the cave,
    and they were so black they couldn't be seen by the evil spirit,

and they perched on the ledges and the rocks.
When the signal was given they all leaped down
    and pecked the evil spirit
    and made such terrible noises
    that they frightened him out into the sunlight.
And like most evil,
    when he hit the sunlight he just melted away
    and disappeared.
They freed the Corn Woman Spirit with their big strong beaks,
    and when she walked out into the sunlight
    the corn of the Cherokees began to grow.
From that day forward, the Great Spirit in the heavens
    would not let her come down in person.
And so it is today.
So when you look out at the cornfields
    and see the stalks of corn
    and their leaves waving in the wind,
    you'll know that the Corn Woman Spirit
    is walking though the fields of today.

Cherokees are unlike the Appalachian people,
    they don't take the raven
    and hang him up on a stick and expect the other ravens to
        deduce,
    "Well I can't go to that field, that raven ate corn and he was
        killed."
That wouldn't stop them.
But the Cherokees give the raven a very special place:
    that he was the one that saved the fields of the Cherokee.
So therefore they feel that if he takes a few kernels of corn, that's ok.
But if the raven is in the field, and an animal comes into the field,
    the crows and the ravens will pitch such a fit
    that the people will know
    that someone is stealing their corn,
so they can go down and chase them away.
So I imagine it's all in the way you look at animals and the circle of
        life
    as to whether they're necessary or need to be destroyed.

The Cherokee saw the importance of all animals and all people
and so therefore they had a very special place.
And that story, I feel, is told to teach those lessons.

›› Ganadí, the Great Hunter, and the Wild Boy

We can just go on and on.
The Cherokees have a lot of stories that they tell.
There's one about a great hunter.
And this word is *ga-na-di* (*Kanati*), which means the great one.
And he would go out every day.
And this must have been very early in the time of creation,
    because he alone would go out and get the meat for the village,
    and no one else had to worry about that.
He would go out for a short while and come back
    with some of the most beautiful venison and beautiful game
    that the people had ever seen.
One day he was down by the river cleaning this venison,
    and all of a sudden a droplet of blood came from the carcass,
    and it fell into the water.
And this droplet of blood represents evil that was introduced—
    sort of like the apple in the Garden of Eden.
This droplet of blood went down the stream,
    and it generated itself
    into a little boy.
And he walked out onto the shores of the river
    and began to play with the hunter's son.
And when the hunter heard them talking—
    he knew his son was supposed to be alone—
    he went over to look, to see who was there with his son,
    and he found this wild boy
    playing with his son.
So when the wild child saw the hunter,
    he ran away into the woods.
So the hunter was concerned about him,
    and he told his son,
    "Well, tomorrow when we come back,

we'll do the same thing.
And when he comes to you,
    you wrestle him to the ground and hold him fast
    so we can tie him up and take him back to the village."
So the next day they went through the same ritual,
    and sure enough,
    the young, wild child came back to them,
    and the hunter's son wrestled him to the ground.
They tied him up and took him back to the village.
So evil was introduced into the village of the people.
And the hunter every day would go
    and do the thing he was supposed to do.
And one day the wild boy told the hunter's son,
    "Where does your father go, every day?"
He said,
    "I don't know.
    My father told me never to follow him."
And so he said,
    "One of these days, your father will die, and we will all starve,
    because we will not know where to go get the food."
So evidently this was the introduction of death
    into the village, also.
He finally talked the hunter's son into following his father.
So one day, when he went to hunt,
    they followed at a distance and watched him go into a swamp.
And he got some beautiful straight reeds,
    made arrow shafts from them.
He got some really nice flint
    and chipped the arrow points out.
They'd never seen this done before.
And so he went on—on the hill—
    and found some feathers that had fallen to the earth,
    and he put them on the arrows.
Made a bow of yellow locust,
    and he walked on up the mountainside.
And so,
    this evil child could change himself into other things—
    he was magical.

So he changed himself into a feather
    and floated in the wind
    and landed on the hunter's shoulder.
He was close enough to see that the hunter had come to a place in
        the mountain
    where there was a big, round rock.
And he rolled the stone back,
    and a deer came running out,
    and he shot it.
And another one,
    and he shot it.
Then he rolled the stone back in place.
So the evil child floated back down the mountainside
    very quickly, as a feather,
    and he changed himself back into a person,
    and they ran back to the village
    before the hunter even knew what had happened.
So the hunter came to clean the deer,
    and these two boys decided
    they would go out and do the same thing he'd done.
They went to the swamp and made their little arrow shafts,
    chipped the stone the best they could,
    and made a bow out of a crooked stick,
    and went up to the mountainside,
    and tugged and tugged upon the round stone,
    and finally got it to roll back enough
    that the animals began to run out of the earth.
They shot at them with all the arrows they had made
    and missed each and every time.
They tried to roll the stone back, but they couldn't.
And all the game in the earth
    ran and spread out all over the earth.
So therefore the Cherokees became hunters and gatherers,
    no longer in the land—
    sort of like the Garden of Eden—
    where they would be taken care of.
And this story takes some strange twists because,
    the two sons are heading back to the village,

and they heard the great hunter coming in their direction.
He had heard all the noise
   of all the animals
   leaving the earth
   and spreading out and flying.
So he had headed back toward the mountain
   to try to roll the stone back in place before they all got out.
One of the boys, the wild child, ran off into the forest.
But the one, the hunter's real son, went back for his punishment.
He told his father what he had done,
   and his father sent him back to the village.
When he got to the stone
   all the animals had run out and flown out,
   and so there was nothing left.
He just left it open as a cave.
But the wild child
   began to try to hunt
   and track down the animals.
And he stayed out in the forest,
   spring
   and all summer long,
   most of the fall.
And then when winter began to come on,
   he began to decide that he needed to go back to the village
   because snows were coming on the mountains.
When he headed back to the village,
   he saw a village way far below
   where people were starving and moaning and wailing.
And so he got closer,
   and he realized—he saw the great hunter there,
   and he was afraid of him,
   that he would be angry with him.
And when he went into the village,
   the great hunter was very glad to see him,
   went over and welcomed him,
   told him that he was the only one that could save the people in
      the village,
   that he had learned to track the animals and hunt the animals,

that he would have to teach the other people how to do that.
And so the great hunter gave him his spears and his bows that he
            had made,
    had him to teach the people
    how to search and hunt for the food.
So it's almost like the story of the Prodigal Son,
    who had done wrong, and he came back, and they were glad to
            see him.
So the Cherokees have a lot of parallels.
When you live life,
    those experiences that you have
    will teach you to have values
    that will produce certain reactions
    in people, in human behavior.
So even though the earth was round,
    and the people were on this side of the earth
    that the Europeans and the Middle East didn't know about,
    things were happening.
They were learning,
    they were teaching their children,
    and they lived for many thousands of years
    in really good cooperation with nature
    and all things that lived around them.
So I think they're to be commended
    for their treatment of things
    on this side of the earth.
Because when the settlers came
    everything was in order.
The trees were beautiful and large, and the great canopies covered
            the forest.
There were no briars or brambles underneath—
    the Cherokees knew how to burn the forests
    and keep them trimmed and groomed correctly.
The fishes of the stream were abundant,
    and the animals in the forest.
The chestnuts were covering the ground,
    sometimes a foot deep.
This is what the settlers found.

And it's because of the way the Cherokees
> told their stories,
> and taught their children,
> and revered the earth itself.
When the settlers came,
> they realized that they must be nature worshipers.
And the people,
> the Cherokees, realized they would not survive without nature,
> but nature was a creation of the Great Spirit,
> so they were thankful to him
> but very appreciative of the nature itself.
Which I think is very, very wise,
> when you look at things today
> and you realize.

≫ The Story of the Bat

Okay. There was a story of a bat.
They say that once there was a dispute between the animals and the
> birds,
> and they were fighting over a certain territory.
And they'd fought for a long time without a great deal of settlement
> of the issue.
And one day the leaders of the group
> decided that they would have a ball game—
> that nothing else was working,
> they were fighting,
> the wars weren't settling anything,
So the ball game could possibly settle the dispute.
So they began to choose their sides.
And the great bear on one side began to choose up his team,
> and the eagle began to choose the side for the birds.
And the bear chose
> the mountain lion and the wolf and the bobcat
> and right on down to the chipmunks
> and felt like his side was complete.
But there was a little animal that had been sort of covered over by
> the leaves,

and he began to run over to the bear,
and he tapped the bear on his big claw.
And the bear looked down,
and he said, "Who are you?"
And he said, "I'm a mouse, and I got left out."
And so the bear laughed,
and he said,
"You're so small you wouldn't be any good to anybody."
So he kicked the little mouse,
and he began to tumble and roll through the leaves
and eventually ended up
underneath the claw of the great eagle.
The eagle looked down,
and he said, "What do you want?"
The little mouse said,
"I'd like to play on your side because the animals don't want me.
The bear has kicked me and mistreated me."
The eagle says,
"Can you fly?"
The little mouse says,
"No, I can't fly."
So the eagle summoned the woodpecker,
and he brought some sycamore bark,
and he had made holes in it with his sharp beak,
and they sewed these pieces of bark underneath—
the wings of the mouse.
And early that morning they began to toss him into the air
and try to teach him to fly.
All day long he would land with a thud upon the ground.
But eventually,
late that evening
just before dark,
the little mouse learned to fly.
And he flew with such precision that he was great.
They began to toss stones at him
and couldn't even hit him,
and he was really, really good.
So the next day

the ball game began to take place.
They went out to the middle of the field
    as it's traditional to do in the stickball game,
    and they all lined up,
    and they threw the ball up into the air.
And all of a sudden—
    they waited for it to come down,
    and they were going to fight and wrestle
    and fight for the ball,
    but it didn't come down.
And they looked,
    and this little creature had gotten the ball
    before it even came back to the ground
    and had taken it back through the goalposts.
Twenty-one times he scored for the birds.
And the birds won the ball game.
And so if you look out today you'll see him
    just before dark,
    flying,
    and he's called the bat.
And there's a great teaching in this story,
    in that
    we should always
    choose all the people
    and not leave out
    those who are smaller.
We should always
    make sure that we don't overlook the feelings of others
    regardless if they're a little bit different than we are.
And I relate this back to when I was teaching school.
There was always a child who was not chosen.
There was always a child who may have been obese.
And they always left this child out.
I think of one in particular.
And every time she would be sitting over on the steps,
    her face was—with great sadness.
But someone was big enough on one of the teams to say,
    "You can come and play with us."

And when she did,
    her face would break into a smile, and she would go out.
And she couldn't run very fast,
    and she couldn't kick very well,
    but sometimes she would kick the ball,
    and one child would act like that they missed it.
And when she ran,
    she would move about as fast
    as most children would when they were walking,
    and they would let her get to first base.
And this was a great gift to her,
    because her smile was very, very happy.
This particular child lived to be about nineteen years old
    and died of a heart disease.
But this goes to prove that we should treat others well,
    and we will not have any regrets
    when *we* get to that point.
So when you're choosing up,
    remember everyone.
This story teaches, I guess I feel like,
    one of the greatest behaviors and values of all,
    and even in Biblical times it was mentioned.
The greatest one is to love God,
    and the second one is like unto it,
    love your brothers and sisters.
So the Cherokees knew that
    even before the settlers came over.
And it's sort of like,
    the old Cherokee chief said it one time,
    "If these people have had this great book so long,
    why can't they treat us better?"

›› The Removed Townhouses

I have probably one more that I'd like to do today.
And this is sort of a revelation-type story in Cherokee history.
And I don't understand exactly how it originated,
    but evidently long before the tragedies of the people happened,

the Cherokees were sitting in a council house.
And you can imagine this big building sitting on top of a mound
    of the ancient mound builders
    with thousands of seats inside.
And they're all gathered in the middle of winter,
    and there's a big fire crackling in the middle of the council.
And the chiefs are all gathered
    in the center,
    at the bottom,
    and the people are listening
    to the oral history being told
    or to the business being discussed.
When all of a sudden
    with no wind whatsoever outside
    the bearskin on the council house opens up
    wide enough for a person to come through
    and then sort of folds back,
    and then all of a sudden
    drops back into place.
The Cherokee, being very superstitious
    as they were in those days,
    realized that someone, some spirit,
    had entered the council house.
So they sat very quietly,
    and sure enough, up in the corner of the council house
    they began to see a light.
A sort of greenish-colored light materialized,
    and it soon turned into a person.
They knew this person was a Cherokee,
    but they didn't know who he was.
He came down to where the chiefs were sitting,
    and he said,
    "You, my brothers and sisters, must follow me.
    For out of the east will come a group of people
    who will destroy your homes.
    And your villages will be burned,
    and your children will be killed,
    and your homeland will be taken away,

and never again will you be happy."
And so the Cherokee said,
    "No, we can't leave,
    because this land belonged to my mothers' mothers' mother."
He said,
    "I'll be back in seven days,
    and you must fast and decide
    whether you'll go with me
    or stay here and suffer."
In seven days he came back again,
    and half of the people had decided to follow him,
    half had decided to stay home.
And so when he came,
    the half that followed him
    went up toward the mountain,
    the sacred mountain of the Cherokee.
And he got to this great massive rock cliff
    and he touched it with his hand,
    and the whole cliff opened up.
And you could hear people singing and laughing inside the
        mountain,
    and a stairwell leading up to a beautiful land
    of springtime and summer.
The people began to march in
    with the butterflies flying,
    and the fruit trees bearing fruit,
    and the people were all happy.
One man at the end
    decided that—he had left his family there in the village,
    and he wanted to go back and get them
    and bring them to this beautiful land.
He rushed back to the village
    and headed back to the mountain.
When he got back to the mountain with his family
    the mountain had closed up,
    and they said he was crazy
    and left him there alone.
He stayed there for seven days,

and on the seventh day
  he began to hear the singing
  deep within the earth.
And so he went back to the village.
And from that day forward
  he told the people in the village
  that if you're quiet enough,
    long enough,
  and if you sit and listen to the streams
  and really are aware
  and very quiet and still,
  that you too can hear the people singing within the earth,
    those happy ones that went on before.
And sure enough, the settlers came,
  and they began to burn the villages
  and take away the land.
And the Cherokee people have been searching
  for that happiness
  they had long, long ago.
Even today, we have things coming into the reservations
  that make the people not so happy.
It never ends.
And I think the teaching of this story
  not only was the fact that there was a revelation
  of what was about to happen—
  people losing their homeland
    on the Trail of Tears and so on.
But also to teach us
  that we should never let the child disappear from us.
You remember when you were a child,
  when you would take off your shoes
  and prod through the mud puddles
  and laugh and sing?
Remember when you were a child,
  that not a butterfly passed
  that you didn't see it and chase it?
And not an animal or an insect were overlooked,
  that you were so close to nature

and so close to Mother Earth
    that those were the things that were important to you?
So as we grow older we began to,
    in this day in time,
    sit in front of the e-mail for hours, the computer screen,
    and we don't know where our children are;
    the rest of our families send their grandparents to the old folks'
        home
    and turn on the TV, a one-sided interaction.
And we should remain like children
    and keep society from choking us and strangling us
    to the point of heart attacks and high blood pressure.
We should remain like children
    and sometimes take our shoes off
    and prod through the mud puddles
    and sit by the streams
    and listen to the talking of the streams
        and the whispers of the wind.
And save ourselves a great deal of medical bills
    and psychological analysis
    and relaxation therapy,
    which costs fifty to a hundred dollars an hour.
Go listen to the stream.
He'll talk to you and will not charge you a penny.
So I think this is Cherokee psychology,
    studied and revised for thousands of years.
I think it's good for all of us.
We must preserve the earth,
    and we must value the lives of our elders
    and the lives of our children
    and save them a place to live.
If we don't
    then there will be a revelation for the people of today
    as well as for the Cherokee.
Thank you.

➤➤ Sources

Books and Articles

Arneach, Lloyd. *The Animal's Ballgame: A Cherokee Story from the Eastern Band.*
Illustrated by Lydia G. Halverson. Chicago: Children's Press, 1992.

Basso, Keith. " 'Stalking with Stories': Names, Places, and Moral Narratives
among the Western Apache." In *Text, Play, and Story: The Construction and
Reconstruction of Self and Society*, 19–55. Proceedings of the American
Ethonological Society, 1983, edited by Stuart Plattner (proceedings editor)
and Edward M. Bruner (editor and symposium organizer). Washington,
D.C.: American Ethnological Society, 1984.

Bell, Corydon. *John Rattling-Gourd of Big Cove: A Collection of Cherokee Indian Legends.*
Written and illustrated by Corydon Bell. New York: Macmillan, 1955.

Bradley, Ramona K. *Weavers of Tales.* Cherokee, N.C.: Qualla Arts and Crafts Co-
op, 1967.

Broun, Emily. *How Rabbit Stole Fire.* Illustrated by Jack Ferguson. New York:
Aladdin Books, 1954.

Bruchac, Joseph. *The First Strawberries: A Cherokee Story.* Retold by Joseph Bruchac,
illustrated by Anna Vojtech. New York: Dial Books for Young Readers, 1993.

Bruchac, Joseph, and Gayle Ross. *The Story of the Milky Way: A Cherokee Tale,* 1st ed.
New York: Dial Books for Young Readers, 1995.

Burrison, John A., ed. *Storytellers: Folktales and Legends from the South.* Athens:
University of Georgia Press, 1989.

Carter, Forrest. *The Education of Little Tree.* Foreword by Rennard Strickland.
Albuquerque: University of New Mexico Press, 1986.

Chiltoskey, Mary Ulmer. *Aunt Mary, Tell Me a Story: A Collection of Cherokee Legends and
Tales.* Cherokee, N.C.: Cherokee Communications, 1991.

Cohlene, Terri. *Dancing Drum: A Cherokee Legend.* Vero Beach, Fla.: Rourke Corp.,
1990.

Crow, Vernon H. *Storm in the Mountains: Thomas' Confederate Legion of Cherokee Indians and Mountaineers*. Cherokee, N.C.: Museum of the Cherokee Indian, 1982.

Cunningham, Keith. *American Indians' Kitchen-Table Stories: Contemporary Conversations with Cherokee, Sioux, Hopi, Osage, Navajo, Zuni, and Members of Other Nations*. Little Rock, Ark.: August House Publishers, 1992.

Duncan, Barbara Reimensnyder. "American Ginseng in Western North Carolina: A Cross-Cultural Examination." In *May We All Remember Well: A Journal of the History and Cultures of Western North Carolina*, edited by Robert Brunk, 201–13. Asheville, N.C.: Robert S. Brunk Auction Services Inc., 1997.

———. "Cherokee Sacred Sites in the Appalachians." In *Cultural Heritage Conservation of the American South*, edited by Benita Howell, 107–18. Southern Anthropological Society Proceedings, no. 23. Athens: University of Georgia Press, 1990.

———. "Going to Water: A Cherokee Ritual in Its Contemporary Context." *Journal of Appalachian Studies* 5 (Spring 1993): 94–100.

———. "Native American Health in the Land That Became North Carolina." *Tar Heel Junior Historian* 36 (Spring 1997): 4–8.

Dundes, Alan. *The Morphology of North American Indian Folktales*. Folklore Fellows Communications, no. 195. Helsinki, Finland: Suomalainen Tiedeakatemia, 1964.

Finger, John H. *Cherokee Americans: The Eastern Band of Cherokees in the Twentieth Century*. Lincoln: University of Nebraska Press, 1991.

Garrett, J. T., and Michael T. Garrett. *Medicine of the Cherokee: The Way of Right Relationship*. Santa Fe, N.M.: Bear and Co., 1996.

Glassie, Henry. *Irish Folk Tales*. New York: Pantheon Books, 1985.

———. *Passing the Time in Ballymenone: Culture and History of an Ulster Community*. Bloomington: Indiana University Press, 1995.

Hymes, Dell. *Foundations in Sociolinguistics: An Ethnographic Approach*. Philadelphia: University of Pennsylvania Press, 1974.

Kilpatrick, Jack Frederick, and Anna Gritts Kilpatrick. "Eastern Cherokee Folktales: Reconstructed from the Field Notes of Frans M. Olbrechts." Anthropological Papers no. 80, *Bureau of American Ethnology Bulletin No. 196*. Washington, D.C.: Smithsonian Institution, 1966.

———. *Friends of Thunder: Folktales of the Oklahoma Cherokees*. Norman: University of Oklahoma Press, 1964.

King, Duane H., ed. *The Cherokee Indian Nation: A Troubled History*. Knoxville: University of Tennessee Press, 1979.

King, Laura H. "The Cherokee Story-Teller: The Red and Green Crayfish." *Journal of Cherokee Studies* 2, no. 2 (Spring 1977): 246–50.

———. "The Cherokee Story-Teller: The Trickster Turtle." *Journal of Cherokee Studies* 1, no. 2 (Fall 1976): 110–13.

———. "The Cherokee Story-Teller: The Ustahli Myth." *Journal of Cherokee Studies* 1, no. 1 (Summer 1976): 55–59.

Mails, Thomas E. *The Cherokee People: The Story of the Cherokees from Earliest Origins to Contemporary Times.* Tulsa, Okla.: Council Oaks Books, 1992.

Mills, Margaret. *Rhetorics and Politics in Afghan Contemporary Storytelling.* Philadelphia: University of Pennsylvania Press, 1991.

Mooney, James. *James Mooney's History, Myths, and Sacred Formulas of the Cherokees: Containing the Full Texts of "Myths of the Cherokee" (1900) and "The Sacred Formulas of the Cherokees" (1891).* Originally published by the Bureau of American Ethnology, 1900. Reprint, with a new introduction by George Ellison. Asheville, N.C.: Historical Images, 1992.

———. *The Sacred Formulas of the Cherokees.* Bureau of American Ethnology, 7th annual report. Washington, D.C.: Government Printing Office, 1891.

———. *The Swimmer Manuscript: Cherokee Sacred Formulas and Medicinal Prescriptions.* Revised, completed, and edited by Frans M. Olbrechts. *Bureau of American Ethnology Bulletin No. 99.* Washington, D.C.: Government Printing Office, 1932.

Orr, Joan Greene, ed. *Fading Voices.* Special edition of the *Journal of Cherokee Studies* 14 (1991).

Price, Richard, and Sandra Price. *Two Evenings in Saramaka.* Chicago: University of Chicago Press, 1991.

Reed, Jeannie, ed. *Stories of the Yunwi Tsunsdi, the Cherokee Little People.* Cherokee, N.C.: Cherokee Communications, 1991.

Reed, Marcelina. *Seven Clans of the Cherokee Society.* Cherokee, N.C.: Cherokee Publications, 1993.

Rockwood, Joyce. *Long Man's Song.* New York: Dell Publishing, 1978.

Ross, Gayle. *How Rabbit Tricked Otter and Other Cherokee Trickster Stories.* Illustrated by Murv Jacob, with a foreword by Wilma Mankiller. New York: HarperCollins, 1994.

———. *How Turtle's Back Was Cracked: A Traditional Cherokee Tale.* Illustrated by Murv Jacob. New York: Dial Books for Young Readers, 1995.

Rossman, Douglas Athon. *Where Legends Live: A Pictorial Guide to Cherokee Mythic Places.* Illustrated by Nancy-Lou Patterson, photographs by William E. Sanderson and Douglas A. Rossman. Cherokee, N.C.: Cherokee Publications, 1988.

Roth, Susan L. *The Story of Light.* New York: Morrow Junior Books, 1990.

Scheer, George F., ed. *Cherokee Animal Tales.* Illustrated by Robert Frankenberg. 2d ed. Tulsa, Okla.: Council Oak Books, 1992.

Siler, Margaret R. *Cherokee Indian Lore and Smoky Mountain Stories.* Edited by Barbara A. McRae, illustrated by James H. McRae. 1938. Reprint. Franklin, N.C.: Teresita Press, 1980.

Spade, Watt, et al. *Cherokee Stories.* Illustrated by Jim Redcorn. Middletown, Conn.: Laboratory of Anthropology, Wesleyan University, 1966. In Cherokee and English, distributed by Carnegie Project, Tahlequah, Okla.

Starr, Emmet. *History of the Cherokee Indians and Their Legends and Folklore.* 1921. Reprint. Tulsa, Okla.: Oklahoma Yesterday, 1979.

Starr, Jean. *Tales from the Cherokee Hills.* Winston-Salem, N.C.: J. F. Blair, 1988.

Tedlock, Dennis. *Finding the Center: Narrative Poetry of the Zuni Indians.* Lincoln: University of Nebraska Press, 1972.

——. "On the Translation of Style in Oral Narrative." In *Toward New Perspectives in Folklore,* edited by Americo Paredes and Richard Bauman, 114–33. Austin: University of Texas Press, 1972.

Underwood, Thomas B. *Cherokee Legends and the Trail of Tears.* Cherokee, N.C.: Cherokee Publications, 1956.

——. *The Story of the Cherokee People.* Cherokee, N.C.: Cherokee Publications, 1961.

Cassette Tapes

Calhoun, Walker. *Sacred Songs of Medicine Lake.* Cherokee, N.C., 1997. Songs, dance music, and banjo.

——. *Where Ravens Roost.* Notes by Michael Kline. Cullowhee, N.C.: Mountain Heritage Center, 1992. Songs and dances.

Littlejohn, Hawk. *Long Man's Song.* Old Fort, N.C.: WoodSong Flutes, 1990. Cherokee flute and stories.

Littlejohn, Kathi Smith. *Cherokee Legends I* and *Cherokee Legends II.* Cherokee, N.C.: Cherokee Communications, 1992. Traditional tales with background music.

To contact the storytellers, call the Cultural Resources Office of the Eastern Band of Cherokee Indians at 1-800-357-2771.

►► Index